PARANOIA QUIZ
Test your fear quotient!

1) What item of clothing may, at any moment, pop you in the eye or provide an all-too-handy attachment for attackers, propellers or fast-moving trains?

   (SUSPENDERS)

2) What clothing accessory may cause ravaged retinas and skin cancer?

   (SUNGLASSES)

3) What common, sudden disorder may lead to insomnia, suffocation, fatal exhaustion and dread?

   (HICCUPS)

4) Fill in the blank: Within one year of your last _____, you will die.

   (BIRTHDAY)

5) What common household item is the underlying cause of more than 20,000 accidents every year?

   (RUGS)

SCORING: Perfect score—you qualify as a Prophet of Doom; one error—you're a promising paranoid; two errors—a fledgling fearling; three errors—watch out, your innocence is showing; four to five errors—you're in big trouble and this book is your only hope.

DON'T BUY A CAR MADE ON MONDAY

Vance Muse

PUBLISHED BY POCKET BOOKS NEW YORK

POCKET BOOKS, a Simon & Schuster division of
GULF & WESTERN CORPORATION
1230 Avenue of the Americas, New York, N.Y. 10020

ISBN: 0-671-83424-X

First Pocket Books printing August, 1980

10 9 8 7 6 5 4 3 2 1

POCKET and colophon are trademarks of Simon & Schuster.

Printed in the U.S.A.

For Vance Sr.

Acknowledgments

Thanks to Melinda Muse, Diane Lowrey,
Donna McCrohan and,
for his idea, Ron Joseph.

Author's Note

My answer to the never-ending news that everything is out to get you is absolutely affirmative. Your favorite food, the sport you like best, hobbies, medicine, work—the very things on which you depend for survival and good times—are not conducive to the continuation of the species. There are, of course, a few harmless pursuits about, but they're also uninteresting: Oatmeal, string-collecting, the mellow sound, and checkers come to mind. The inventory of things to avoid, flee, and fear is expanding, so the least you can do is develop a knowing relationship with your animate and inanimate adversaries. How and why you're endangered as never before is what this book endeavors to explain.

Behaviorists say that fears are learned, so consider this a textbook, the only one to own. You may already tremble at black widow spiders, lightning, red dye no. 2, and terrorists, but here you'll learn to be wary of rings, oleanders, soccer fans, manhood, umbrellas, and CB radios—all of which can hurt, maim, or kill, as can bacon, retirement, yoga, and ballpoint pens.

This selective register of life's obvious and obscure dangers will specify those vague rumblings you've had for years, fears you perhaps thought were unfounded, fears that made you seem paranoid. Paranoia is the point: How else to get from year to year if not shaky, skittish, and suspicious? The Cowardly Lion had the right idea, and would appreciate this manual for proud paranoids, this encyclopedia of panophobia, this guidebook for timorous consumers.

While burdening you with facts and outrages and lore and opinions, these caveats, which range from a couple of lines to a few paragraphs, will vindicate poltroons and convert the arrogant or oblivious who pride themselves on having experienced no trepidation. The idea is that the world is ludicrously dangerous, so you'd best yield, exercise caution, get those hands up. Whether you wave the white flag with dignified resignation or total panic, the important thing is that you do surrender.

It's not too late to knuckle down and bone up on your founded fears (and have a good time doing it). They're all here: things you shouldn't touch; what you shouldn't do; how not to do it; where you mustn't go; who not to cross; when it's not safe. What you should be afraid of—and why.

A

AEROSOLS

People use aerosols to deodorize themselves, clean windows, repel insects, clean ovens, do their hair, paint things, wax furniture, clean walls, grease pans—even to apply a cheeselike substance to crackers. For many years, fluorocarbons were used as aerosol propellant, but after much evidence was seen and heard of their attack on ozone and their ability to raise temperatures by absorbing infrared radiation in the troposphere, fluorocarbons have been banned from the cans and replaced by hydrocarbons. It's not much of an improvement, for the hydrocarbons used are the same flammable ones found in stoves, lanterns, and cigarette lighters—namely, butane, isobutane, and propane.

"Home and Family Maintenance Products," many of them jettisoned through aerosols, rank high on the hazard index of the Consumer Product Safety Commission. The main problem with the new hydrocarbon propellants is their volatility, especially when those containers are stored near hot-water pipes under sinks. Because the contents are greatly pressurized with the hydrocarbon propellant, they can explode, doing obvious damage to eyes and skin. (*See* COSMETICS, HOME.)

AIR

Air isn't looking or smelling very good at all, and it's not going to get any better, not with the revival of coal, the automobile's tenacity, and diesel fuel's acceleration. It is not unheard-of for some cities to report unacceptable air quality 320 days a year; Los Angeles, Detroit, Denver,

New York, Houston, Philadelphia, and Albuquerque are particularly polluted, and harmful air, of course, doesn't stay put—easterners, for example, inhale pollutants expelled from refineries in the midwest.

Great clouds of carbon dioxide produced by the renewed reliance on coal and continued production of other fossil fuels have the ultimate effect of trapping solar heat—which means we'll either burn to a crisp or be drowned in melted glaciers. Fossil fuels are also responsible for atmospheric sulfates and nitrates, which return to earth as acid rainfall. Depending on its concentration, the acidic deluge kills vegetation and fish on contact, destroys works of art, corrodes buildings, and renders soil sterile.

As sources of pollution, the world's refineries, power plants, and smelters can't compete with cars, buses, and trucks. In New York City, vehicles account for 95 percent of carbon monoxide, 65 percent of hydrocarbon, 40 percent of nitrous oxide, and 50 percent of photo-chemical pollution. The news gets worse as individuals, transit systems, and taxi-cab companies turn to diesel for better mileage: Preliminary experiments with the fuel show that it emits up to 80 times the particulates and cancer-causing hydrocarbons of regular gasoline.

Whatever their source, the major air pollutants—ozone, sulfur dioxide, carbon monoxide, nitrogen oxides, and hydrocarbons—cause enormous health problems. Not surprisingly, these are mostly respiratory: asthma, bronchitis, emphysema. Children, being pure of lung, are thought to be most vulnerable to bad air, though it is also known to aggravate older people's heart diseases, decrease anyone's ability to effectively exercise, and cause premature death of many ill patients who require copious amounts of fresh oxygen.

While gas masks may save the lungs, there's not much you can do to prevent caustic air from irritating skin and burning eyes. (*See* COAL, EATING SNOW.)

ALCOHOL

Prohibition probably wasn't such a bad idea:

—Ninety million Americans drink, eleven million of them too much.

—Half of all murder victims had been drinking before their number came up.

—Alcohol stimulates a liver enzyme that interferes with testosterone, thereby impairing men's sexual functioning.

—More than half of the people who die in car wrecks, and half of all other fatal accident victims, have alcohol in their blood at the time of death.

—One third of all suicides are related to alcohol consumption.

—There are more teenaged drinkers than ever before, and 61 percent of them drink to drunkenness once a month.

—Alcohol is the most common cause of convulsions.

—Alcohol makes you urinate frequently, which involves a lot of time in the most dangerous room in the house.

As it's drunk, alcohol first irritates the mouth and throat membranes, then is absorbed pronto, essentially in its original form, since the body can't make it chemically more acceptable as it does virtually every other ingested substance. Most of the absorption takes place not in the stomach but in the intestine where, unfortunately, it happens faster. From there, alcohol enters the bloodstream to make poisonous acetaldehyde in the liver and anesthetize the brain as it destroys its cells. After a smaller amount than most people think, the drinker begins to talk funny, look pitiful, and become obnoxious and dangerous.

Switching to a less potent brew doesn't help much, for though it is true that beer is less alcoholic than gin, it is usually imbibed in greater quantity. (Beer is dangerous for other reasons—keep reading.)

AMBULANCE SERVICE

Accidents account for most deaths during the first half of life. A third of traffic fatalities occur at the scene, in ambulances, or within one minute of arrival at emergency rooms. One would hope, therefore, for speedy and efficient ambulance service. Dream on.

Many of the emergency vehicles on the road are poorly maintained heaps and, sadder still, there aren't enough, even of them.

Studies have shown that ambulances are sometimes without basics such as antiseptics, burn sprays, splints, bandages, even tire-changing tools.

Ambulance crews are not what you'd call expert—many are untrained to treat shock, hemorrhage, broken bones, or even to extricate victims from wreckage.

Ambulance company headquarters are often located in remote parts of town, and sometimes require an hour to get to the victims and take them on to the hospital.

That is, if they make it that far. Ambulance services are owned and operated by hospitals, police and fire departments, private firms, volunteer organizations, and especially in rural areas, funeral homes. Think about it: Do morticians want survivors? Ambulance drivers have accepted tips from funeral directors for delivering dead (or dying) bodies to their dark doorsteps. Accident casualties have died while drivers from competing ambulance companies haggled over their fractured bodies. And though speed is essential to rescue, many drivers use it as an excuse to go joy riding.

Deficient ambulance service is blamed by some medical insiders for about 20,000 deaths per year in the United States. Things won't get better until government regulations and standards for emergency services are set up and strictly enforced. As it is, when an ambulance is called you're in for about an hour's wait in large towns and cities, and a trip to the funeral parlor in small towns.

ANESTHESIA

The quest for the ideal anesthetic is at least as old as the search for aphrodisiacs, just as futile, and proves the popular prejudice against pain. Hypnotism, acupuncture, electrical currents, and radio waves have been used to allay surgical agony, but drugs are the preferred anesthetic agents. Local, spinal, or general, they are usually administered after a strong sedative, and may be such volatile liquids as ether and chloroform; nitrous oxide, halothane, and cyclopropane gases; or injectable barbiturates, sodium pentothal being the most widely used general anesthetic. Endotracheal intubation of gas risks tearing delicate throat tissues and suffocation, but anesthetic injection is more dangerous, a virtual mainlining into the central nervous system. Depending on the anesthetist (most often unknown to the anesthetized), a combination of substances and techniques will be used to get the patient into a cadaverous state of consciousness.

All anesthetics depress the central nervous system, stifle protest to pain, and have been responsible for allergies, destruction of body tissues, liver and kidney damage, and circulatory and respiratory slowdown. Until these side effects came to light, the chief danger associated with anesthetics was operating-room explosion. In the 1940s, flammable ether caused as many as 60 explosions per week in U. S. hospitals.

Ether and cyclopropane are rarely used today, and fortunately so: They can cause violent nausea and vomiting. Nitrous oxide is short-acting, so must be administered over a long period of time, and the prolonged exposure can interfere with the bone marrow's manufacture of disease-fighting white blood cells. Spinal anesthetics, known as neuromuscular blockers, are derived from curare, developed by South American hunters for poisoning darts intended for big game, a fact that could make you settle for biting a bullet. Even seemingly harmless Novocaine can be misinjected, and if a dentist hits the wrong nerve the patient may be permanently palsied.

General anesthetics stupefy the cerebral cortex, and the aftershocks range from an inability to urinate to amnesia. Anesthetic overdoses and allergies have killed patients before surgeons even raised their scalpels. (*See* DOCTORS, HYPNOSIS.)

ANTACID

Antacid abuse may not be the most upsetting of social problems (it is societal because of its ties to stress and gastronomic indulgence), but is serious nonetheless, leading to phosphate depletion, fatigue, and vitamin D deficiency.

ANTHROPOPHAGY

Charles Grodin: What animals are you afraid of?
Louise Lasser: The ones that can eat me.
CG: That's smart.
LL: But I'm scared of everything.
CG: You sure don't show it.
LL: I'm too scared to.

From "Just Me and You," an original screenplay by Louise Lasser, copyright © 1978 by Louise Lasser.

Whacking your way into interior New Guinea is one sure way to get eaten by your fellow man, but anthropophagy, or cannibalism, really isn't that remote. It has been practiced by various peoples on most continents throughout history, and fashions, tastes, and the food industry being what they are, cannibalism might make a comeback—depending on dictate, whim, or necessity.

People eat people for what they consider the sheer delicacy of human flesh, or in seeking to absorb a person's vitality or wisdom. (The latter usually entails ingesting only certain organs—no comfort to the eaten.)

The Kwakiutl Indians of the northwestern coast of the United States practiced cannibalism as a ritual of their secret societies. Some cannibals encourage reciprocity, believing it better to be eaten by friends than worms.

APPENDECTOMIES

Research indicates that people who've had their vermiform appendixes removed develop a propensity to a whole series of diseases.

ARGUING

You'll live longer by acquiescing. A murder is committed about every 27 minutes, and 72 percent of them are the result of some kind of disagreement.

ARTIFICIAL TURF

Games played on artificial turf are more dangerous than the same games played on grass, no matter how dirty or rocky the real stuff might be.

Certain bacteria that thrive in the artificial turf compound scratches and cuts suffered by athletes.

Turf generally tends to be slippery. Since its invention in 1965, ankle injuries peculiar to the turf and "rug burns" have plagued players.

The synthetic playing surface also holds heat, increasing the temperatures in some stadiums as much as 30°F.—and that raises the possibility of heat exhaustion and stroke.

ASPHALT

Highways, driveways, and runways are commonly topped with asphalt, which is fine if the sun's not beating down, for summer heat can turn the bituminous blacktop into a virtual quicksand, a gooey threat to anything on wheels.

Then there are times when asphalt isn't soft enough. Playground accidents—there are at least 120,000 every year in the United States—would be less abrasive if, when kids fall from swings, slides, and seesaws, they could land on surfaces with more give than asphalt, which has been thoughtlessly used on recreational areas throughout the country.

ASPIRIN

To live by medicine is to live horribly.   —*Linnaeus*

Funny how we think of drug abuse: Ten percent of adverse drug reactions and most accidental poisonings are related to aspirin, yet it's available to anyone, anywhere. Plain old aspirin is the most widely used medicine in the world (Americans spend $500 million annually on the drug) and it can cause rashes, asthma, anemia, nausea, and stomach bleeding.

American Indians discovered that chewing willow bark would relieve various discomforts, and the bark's medicinal ingredient, salicylic acid, was isolated by British doctors in 1860. In 1899, the Bayer company of Germany came up with a substance called acetyl-salicylic acid, which contained the pain-relieving qualities of sodium salicylate, the sodium salt of salicylic acid that had been sold in European apothecaries in the late nineteenth century. Bayer called its new compound aspirin, and it was only a slight refinement of the Indian's raw willow bark. Aspirin enjoyed instant success, met with immediate competition, and is today the first drug we reach for to fight headaches, colds, fever, and rheumatoid arthritis.

The medical community was on to aspirin's side effects by the 1920s but, according to *Saturday Review,* they weren't made public until 1968, when a U.S. astronaut was dropped from the space program due to what newspapers headlined his "rare disease"—aspirin intolerance. The astronaut's experience with aspirin was a severe respiratory one, and hundreds of people have now identified their wheezing and gasping as aspirin intolerance which, like any allergy, may develop at any time in life. Aspirin often contains a contaminating substance, aspirin anhydride, that's responsible for hives.

Aspirin's most dangerous side effect is internal bleeding, caused by its stomach-stinging acetic and salicylic acids. Aspirin has also been shown to inhibit blood clotting.

So before you take two with a glass of water, maybe you ought to visit an allergist. And keep some antacid nearby (even though it's dangerous, too).

ASTROLOGY

Astrologists haven't come up with any new ideas since 100 B.C., when the reading of horoscopes was first devised. That astrology has not changed with the times is probably the very basis of its appeal, a disturbing fact when you consider that many people make life-and-death decisions according to astrologists' money-making interpretations of zodiacal influences.

The pseudoscience is founded on a presumptuous and meaningless division of the heavens into twelve houses. Even so, astrologists enjoy great and loyal followings; they could convince their faithful to do very foolish things—move to Australia, say, or buy cars manufactured on Monday.

ATKINS, SUSAN D.

Susan D. Atkins is serving a life term in Frontera, California, for stabbing and torturing to death eight people at the behest of Charles Manson on August 9, 1969. She was 21 at the time.

Atkins talked a lot to her cellmates. Vincent Bugliosi and Curt Gentry quote her in *Helter Skelter*.

Atkins on murder: "You have to have a real love in your heart to do this for people."

On stabbing: "It feels good when the knife goes in."

On blood: "It's warm and sticky and nice."

So far, she's been denied parole.

AUSTRALIA

The koala bear just isn't worth the trip, not with so much else there that can kill you. Australia's like a hostile planet in a sci-fi novel: Kangaroos are neat to look at, but can punch you out; a disproportionate number of venomous snakes crawl the continent; and the cassowary, a huge hysterical bird, pounces on people. There's even a rather large spider there whose web can trap children. Australia's waters contain 27 species of sea snakes, man-eating sharks, the dreaded saltwater crocodile, the world's most poisonous fish, vicious crabs, moray eels, and the deadliest of all jellyfish. We'll examine a few here since you won't read about them in travel brochures.

First, that bird. Cassowaries, tall and distant relatives of the ostrich, are flightless, which by no means lessens their impact. Australian and New Guinean natives report just how badly humans lose when an annoyed cassowary attacks: The bird has a way of leaping into the air and slashing down with its long claws, powerful enough to halve a man.

Sixty percent of Australia's land snakes are poisonous and numbering among them are the formidable tiger snake (the world's deadliest, many herpetologists say) and the taipan, whose venomous bite penetrates tough shoe leather. Only India and South America report more snakebites than Australia.

Crocodiles, unsubtle evidence of our Age of Reptiles, are by nature man-eaters, and get on smoothly in or out of water. Their dining technique is gruesome: Unlike snakes, they cannot swallow large prey, so must dismember their victim by first chomping then twirling. Australia's giant salt-water crocodiles are quite adept at this violence and are known to have so devoured hundreds of men.

Most people think the Portuguese-man-o-war is the worst jellyfish to encounter, but Australia's less famous sea wasp is profoundly more deadly. One barb from the long tentacles of this jellyfish, and you're in a real jam. Unlike other jellyfish, the sea wasp's venom is neurotoxic, and results in violent local reactions and permanent scars; their stings are so severe that in deep water a victim may drown before he knows what's hit. In Darwin, Australia, in 1938, a 12-year-old boy could barely make it to the beach after being stung; once he did, he fell dead.

Closer to shore and only on the east coast, lies the most poisonous fish in the world, the stonefish. Perfectly camouflaged by craggy rocks and dark coral (they are also the world's ugliest marine animal), stonefish hold a venom in their steely spines whose power is beyond belief. A single puncture will have you praying for death; the pain is so intense that morphine doesn't help. After stepping on a stonefish, people are known to collapse, scream wildly, and froth at the mouth. Sickness from the poison may linger for a year, and the stung appendages— usually toes or fingers—often turn black and fall off.

Now that's what Qantas doesn't tell you. (*See* SNAKES, WATER.)

B

BAIKAL—AMUR MAINLINE RAILWAY

"BAM," the Soviet railway that plows across the snows and ice of northern Siberia, will open in 1983, but don't plan on riding it. Its 2,000 miles cut through some of the most forbidding terrain and temperatures (as low as 50°F. below zero) on the planet. BAM's tracks sit on earthquake zones, and are supported along the glacial way by 3,700 bridges.

BALLOONING

A sheep, a rooster, and a duck were the first hot-air balloon passengers, and only one, the duck, belonged up there. Under the supervision of the balloon's inventors, Joseph and Jacques Montgolfier, the noisy trio was lifted to a height of 1,500 feet. King Louis XVI witnessed the event and was enthralled, but showed rare good sense in choosing not to go up himself. French scientist J. F. Pilatre de Rozier, encouraged by his first manned balloon ride in 1783 (the same year as the animals' ascent), continued experimenting until his hydrogen balloon ignited in the sky, at which point he became ballooning's first fatality—but by no means its last. To this day, the bugaboo of balloons is as it was 200 years ago: They can catch fire, explode, or be hurtled to earth by harsh weather. Too, there is always the risk of oxygen deprivation as one achieves greater altitudes.

The ride is no doubt a thrill, and the balloons themselves are wonderful to look at, but the same can be said for a lot of things that can hurt you. (*See* FLYING, HANG GLIDING, SKYDIVING.)

BALLPOINT PENS

Ballpoint pens make formidable weapons; they should, in fact, be regarded as knives that write. One accident in Japan tells why: A motorcyclist could have walked away from a minor collision had he not been stabbed to death by the ballpoint pen he kept in his front pocket.

BEER

America's favorite bar drink causes cancer. Aflatoxin is a natural chemical produced by molds that grow on the grains used to make beer. It is poisonous (12,000 turkeys died in England after eating aflatoxin-contaminated grain) and a potent cancer-causing substance. It also grows on peanuts, making peanut butter a very dangerous food.

BIRTHDAYS

You will die within a year of your last birthday. That's how it always is. It's as if the breath of life is expended huffing and puffing at birthday candles.

BLACK HOLES

Anything entering a black hole—a collapsed star or stars—is sucked into a vortex where space and time and communication make no earthly sense and matter is crushed to its infinite density, an unpleasant fate for anyone.

Not even light can escape black holes, which can be many kilometers in diameter. The menace is growing: Astronomers have found a black hole in Scorpio, and more will surely be discovered out there. (*See* SPACE FLIGHT.)

BLIZZARDS

Extreme cold kills more people in the United States than any other natural event, and there's no expression of extreme cold quite like a blasting blizzard. The very word bodes onomatopoetically, a blizzard being a blitz of blinding snow.

Blizzards are particularly hard on cities, where the white blights freeze public services and utilities as effectively as municipal strikes. Blizzards bring traffic to a halt, destroy power lines, and block access to food supplies and hospitals. And it's not easy to recover from them. It took Buffalo a full year to pull out of the blizzards of 1976. (*See* CITIES.)

BOSTON

The tallest building in New England at sixty-two stories, Boston's John Hancock Tower began rejecting its windows shortly after its construction was completed in 1972. Huge aprons were cantilevered from the building's middle and nearby streets were closed on windy days, protective measures which may account for the lack of many serious injuries. Great rectangles of plywood were first used to replace the errant windows, until a $6,000,000 decision was made to replace all 10,344 of them. Even with the 18.5 acres of new glass, the sad skyscraper inspires fear—gusty days can make a hard-hat out of any Bostonian.

BOTULISM

1971 was bad for soup, being the year of that well-publicized poisoning of a New York banker who died 28 hours after eating canned Bon Vivant vichyssoise. The canned product had cultivated botulin, a toxin so potent that a little glassful could kill every man, woman, and child on earth. *Clostridium botulina* are totally harmless bacteria (fresh fruits and vegetables are crawling with them) until they get tough by germinating in an airless environment, such as a jar or can. There are many possible hosts of botulin: It can grow in green beans, mushrooms, raw honey, olives, chicken, and lots of other foods that aren't high in salt, sugar, or acid. A decade before the banker's bout with botulism, tainted tuna bore the spores and killed two Michigan women.

The toxin seizes control of the nervous system, and paralyzes the respiratory apparatus, often the esophagus. Botulism is now suspected in "crib death," the mysterious incidence where babies just stop breathing.

Botulism should make you generally fearful of swollen canned goods, for that bloatedness may be caused by the pushy gases of a deadly brew.

BUGS

They outnumber us, to say the least. Entomologists can't even grasp their amazing abundance and, hard as we've tried with our idiotic application of pesticides, we've not managed to exterminate a single one of millions of species. In fact, insects are really on the march these days, hardier for their inherited resistance to the ever-stronger poisons of agribusiness. Insects have established themselves as the dominant form of life on earth: They are powerful in their armor-like exoskeletons; they can live in a wide range of temperatures (the adaptable cockroach is equally at home in your oven or refrigerator); they fly, or crawl up, down, and upside-down; they're outlandishly reproductive; they possess highly-developed senses. Clearly, bugs are made for life on this planet.

Although we have allies in the gorgeous, grotesque world of bugs, our enemies there are formidable, particularly killer bees, fire ants, locusts, black-widow spiders, and mosquitoes.

Killer bees lead the swarm of the hymenoptera order of stinging insects whose members—yellow jackets, hornets, wasps, and ants—have killed more people than snakes have. Killer bees are a relatively new menace, the mobile progeny of African killer bees and honeybees of European origin, accidentally bred in Brazil by chagrined scientists. These winged bullets are now buzzing northward, leaving cattle and men dead in the Amazon delta.

The venom from hymenoptera burns fiercely, causing swelling, itching, hives, and anxiety. In a severe reaction, the stings cause labored breathing, difficulty in swallowing, chest constriction, abdominal pains, nausea, rapid fall in blood pressure, and unconsciousness. Death, more likely in victims over 30, can come within 10 minutes. Killer bees are by far the most ferocious winged insects, and since they attack in great numbers, piranha-style, we don't stand a chance with them.

Nor are we much better off with flying fire ants, another unplanned and unwelcome import from South America. The Department of Agriculture says the ants entered through the port of Mobile, Alabama, around 1920, now inhabit millions of acres in 13 southern states, and advance another 25 miles each year. Fire ants have bad tempers, mean jaws, and a wicked poison; they've made corpses of squirrels, pigs, chickens, calves, and people. Fire ants are also dangerous to the economy: Their huge mounds can actually destroy farm machinery and block cultivation of land.

The Book of Joel gives a rather awesome description of locust swarms:

> A day of darkness and of gloominess, a day of clouds and of thick darkness . . . the land is as the garden of Eden before them, and behind them a desolate wilderness . . . nothing can escape them . . . The earth shall quake before them; the heavens shall tremble: the sun and the moon shall be dark.

These huge Biblical bugs, dragons in miniature, must be feared for the utter devastation they bring to this planet. As a locust swarm darkens the sky, its billion members set their incredibly efficient jaws on all vegetation in sight, as during the plague in Sansi, China, which left 6 million persons starving. Locusts are not known to fly *around* anything—they've caused planes to crash, and might eat your soft parts. For this reason, avoid South America, Africa, and the Near East, where they are most given to their capricious mass migrations. (The 1978 plague over the American Plains definitely ranks with the worst; it required a scale of pesticide warfare that was itself a threat to all living things.)

Spiders, closely related to insects, are all venomous, but none quite like the black widow. She is found all over the world, with California reporting the most bites. The pain of those bites can be excruciating, causing hysteria in some people. One victim, bitten on the foot, said it felt like her toenails were being torn off. After the pain subsides somewhat come fever, muscular aches, nausea, dizziness, and paralysis. Death may follow about a week after the bite, most often in children and older people.

We have Thomas Crapper to thank for the decline in black widow bites, for it was his invention of the flush toilet that got us out of the spider's nesting site, the outhouse.

Mosquitoes do not inhabit Antarctica, and that's the only good thing to be said about all 2,500 species of them. The mosquito, with its nasty blood-sucking probiscus, is the world's leading disease carrier, and its bacterial baggage includes yellow fever, encephalitis, malaria, and a dozen others. Malaria, transmitted by mosquitoes' saliva, has wiped out civilizations, caused more American casualties in the South Pacific during World War II than enemy action, and continues to kill a million people each year.

Pesticides

We're in a fine fix, because here's a solution that's proved to be worse than the problem. Which will get us first, the voracious bugs or our pesticide warfare, which amounts to a sort of mass suicide? The thing to keep in mind is that pesticide abuse is not confined to the heartland's great golden fields; industry and home use mightily contribute to the lethal chemical residue. Though pesticides have been banned left and right, it is probably too late—their use has already endangered species and caused genetic damage and cancer in humans.

It all started in 1939 with the development of DDT, which everyone thought was the bee's knees until three discoveries were made: The chlorine-based pesticide was killing useful bugs; the breeding of DDT-resistant insects was underway; and the poison had moved up the food chain, weakening bird eggs and piling up in human tissues. In short order, aldrin, chlordane, hectachlor, and other deadly chlorine derivatives were concocted, and World War II's nerve gas research led to a series of phosphorus-based insecticides. While less environmentally persistent than their chlorine predecessors, the phosphorus sprays, particularly parathion and malathion, are more immediately dangerous to humans—they can kill on contact. Another deadly substance, kepone, has been banned, though it is still with us. Is it ever: Its remaining supplies have been dumped, along with arsenic, cyanide, and mercury, in an abandoned West German salt mine. The mine now holds over 200,000 tons of poisonous wastes—enough, should it escape, to wipe out the world's population.

Insects will continue to develop immunity to new pesticides, a genetic process aided by the industry and government's failure to brew specific solutions for specific bugs. It is more economical, no matter how temporary the benefits, for manufacturers to sell pesticides that kill generally. The chemical arsenal, then, will eventually be exhausted, and the planet will be overrun by immune insects while what remains of pesticides resides in fish and wildlife, grains, and our own fat. (*See* THE FOOD CHAIN.)

Arthropod "birth control," which entomologists say is our only hope, involves tampering with the creatures' hormones and genes with the conceivable result of new species of monstrous and ultimately indestructible insects.

BULL-RIDING

Cowboys have ridden rodeos since 1888, and there's hardly an event in the raucous contests that doesn't risk life and limb. Bruises are the least a man or woman can expect from tackling cattle and wrestling pigs—and the safety of spectators is jeopardized when the rightfully enraged animals attempt to flee arenas.

Bulls have great strength, bad tempers, and horns, and outweigh big men by a ton. That's why bull-riding, according to the National Sportswriters Association, is the most dangerous sport in America.

BURNED TOAST

The black stuff on burned toast is carbon, and it is easily absorbed by the blood, where it can do damage similar to that of other organic carbon-based poisons, including narrowing the arteries, which can lead to heart attack. If the bread burns long enough in the toaster, it will eventually produce lethal carbon monoxide.

C

CB RADIO

CB radio is one more medium by which people keep in touch, and, it turns out, arrange brief encounters for the quick transmission of germs. "CB-VD" is in the medical books as any sort of venereal disease contracted by people who make their sexual pickups over the radios. It's particularly problematic because they tend not to use their real names but their CB "handles"—and those infected good buddies are hard to track down out on the highway. (*See* MICROWAVES.)

CAINISM

Cainism is a religious sect named after the man who was, as the Bible has it, the first murderer. "Cains" think what Cain did to his brother was glorious. (*See* FAMILY AND FRIENDS.)

CALIFORNIA

California will not simply fall into the ocean. Nothing so gentle. The big quake, which geologists have been expecting to rip through the state since the 1950s, is more likely to blast everything between and including San Francisco and Los Angeles clear across the Pacific. The longer the pressures build, the worse it'll be. (*See* TECTONICS.)

The landscape of California is so breathtaking that it distracts motorists. Since all Californians are motorists, this beauty portends another natural disaster.

The state is overrun with black widow spiders (*see* BUGS), and rabid skunks and bats—and reports an alarming number of leprosy cases.

Californians cotton to new products with alarming alacrity. Take hot tubs, for example. In 1979, ten people died by drowning, falling or electrocution in the torrid tubs, and the intense temperatures of the water can cause brain damage in unborn babies.

CAMPING

Reverting to the great outdoors to sleep in bags alongside rattlesnakes—"camping," it's called—titillates people who remain unimpressed by the development of shelter in our evolutionary history. Camping is silly, and so fraught with danger that no hotel room is too great a price to pay to avoid having to do it. All year, though, even when it's freezing, millions of atavistic Americans swarm onto camping grounds (often crowding the animals out) to tempt wild beasts, brush against poisonous plants, risk food poisoning, and misuse equipment.

Grizzly and black bears are always hungry and grouchy and will just as well eat an arm as a graham cracker. Lewis and Clark warned that the bears are "creatures of extraordinary ferocity," something to keep in mind upon entering national parks, where they've dragged men out of sleeping bags and tents. Polar bears are ragingly carnivorous, and not at all shy about approaching people; the Arctic, therefore, rates as a particularly foolish place to commune with nature, as campers say.

The woods are also full of plants that can scratch, stab and kill. I doubt if anyone but the most diligent boy scout can spot poison ivy, not to mention the other leafy menaces, that sensible people, with roofs over their heads, avoid.

The favorite foods of campers—hardboiled eggs, American cheese, potato salad, franks, and other portable culinary underachievements are, alas, attractive to salmonella, the bacteria that cause food poisoning. To discourage bacterial growth, foods must be kept either hot or cold, something not all campers can afford to do.

Fancy equipment is no guarantee of hazard-free outings, however. Gas tanks explode, lanterns and stoves start fires, portable toilets collapse, and stubborn zippers trap people in sleeping bags. Even a simple charcoal stove's flames dance with danger. Smoldering charcoal gives off a heavy concentration of carbon monoxide, and without proper ventilation can fill cabin or tent with the odorless, invisible, and lethal gas.

There might be a point in its favor if aficionados could say that camping takes one far from city nastiness. But this is not the case. Parks, beaches, and other campgrounds are experiencing pollution and an alarming increase in crime. There were nearly 8,000 homicides, rapes, burglaries, larcenies, and car thefts at Yosemite National Park in 1977. (*See* BUGS, DUMB CANE, JULY AND AUGUST, LIGHTNING, MUSHROOMS, OLEANDERS, SNAKES, SPELUNKING, SURVIVAL COURSES, ZIPPERS.)

CARS MANUFACTURED ON FRIDAY AND MONDAY

> I figure that you haven't got any intelligence if you haven't got fear.   —*"Crash" Kavanagh, Stuntman*

Lemons are more likely to roll off the assembly line on Friday and Monday than any other days of the week. No surprises here: The spirit of "TGIF," Monday hangovers, and the resulting absenteeism on both days result in factory follies and endangered motorists.

CENTRAL HEATING AND COOLING

Think how easy it would be to sabotage a central air system. One shot of cyanide gas at its source would be efficiently vented throughout a house or building. Better use window air conditioners and fireplaces.

CHICKEN KIEV AND OMELETS

A few conglomerates dominate domestic poultry production, and supermarket demands keep them hatching at a pace ultimately detrimental to the quality of the hens and eggs. The ubiquitous agribusiness chicken (you have to visit a country store or pay outrageous sums for yard birds and their eggs) lives in a cramped cage, its movement so restricted that its talons may grow into the mesh flooring. The poor creature is exposed to artificial light for the better part of the day and is fed a terrible mix of minerals, hormones, antibiotics, excrement-based organic matter, and chemicals, all to accelerate the bird's growth and laying. The eggs are smaller, with paler yolks and much less flavor than an unadulterated chicken's, and are often chemically contaminated. The days of the happy barnyard hen, scratching for all kinds of earthly goodies, are virtually gone—and with them, tasty and nutritious poultry products.

CHLAMYDIA TRACHOMATIS

This unfriendly microbe is the main cause of the most common venereal disease in developed countries, nongonococcal urethritis, or NGU, and it's even more epidemic than gonorrhea, with which it is often confused.

NGU produces howlingly painful urination, may result in sterility, and, in women, inflammation of the cervix and fallopian tubes—which in turn can cause eye infection and pneumonia in unborn babies.

CHRISTMAS

Christmas, unlike the Fourth of July or even Thanksgiving, is a holiday hard to ignore, and if you're not into the swing of things, all the festivities are liable to make you sick or sad: Thay's why the suicide rate jumps during late December.

Christmas is also dangerous for other reasons:

—Poinsettias, the red Christmas flowers whose petals are sometimes seen leering from bowls of eggnog, carry a sap that can be fatal. Mere handling of the poisonous poinsettia can actually blister the skin and burn eyes.

—Christmas provides the perfect opportunity for juvenile delinquents to pose as carolers: No sooner would these seeming cherubs begin "God Rest Ye Merry, Gentlemen" than they've carted off your television set.

—Wrapping paper sometimes contains lead and chromium, which release toxic fumes when incinerated.

—Christmas tree trimmings are themselves trimmed with TRIS, the carcinogenic flame-retardant. (*See* TRIS.)

—Nibbling all day on room-temperature foods such as turkey stuffing, eggnog, cream pies, and cold-cuts risks food poisoning by salmonella bacteria. (*See* WOODEN CUTTING BOARDS.)

—Families and friends tend to cluster at Christmastime. (*See* FAMœ ILY AND FRIENDS.)

—Icy roads cause car wrecks, but these at least prevent the usage of dangerous gifts—various toys, foods, scarfs and neckties that strangle, digital watches.

THE CIRCUS

The Big Top is full of horrors:

—angry, humiliated elephants;
—collapsible grandstands;
—an amazing array of junk food (*see* SWEETS);
—those bizarre performers who want to lure you away from home;
—human cannonballs who overshoot their nets.

Circuses also assault the sinuses with more things than you can sneeze at: animal hairs, dust, sawdust, animal deodorants, feed.

Along the midway, watch out for those rides that offer all the sensations of space flight with none of the precautions afforded astronauts.

CITIES

For maximum effect, terrorists execute their maneuvers in cities, which are, to the demented liberationists, ideal sites for bombings, kidnappings, ambushes and assassinations. But generally, cities are no worse—or won't be for long—than their suburbs. (For the record, the standard Metropolitan Statistical Areas with populations over one million reporting the highest murder rates in 1978 were New Orleans with 23.8 per 100,000 people; Houston, 23.5; Los Angeles, 17.4; Miami, 17; New York, 16.8; Dallas–Fort Worth, 16.3; Detroit, 15.2; San Antonio, 14.9; St. Louis, 14.4; Atlanta, 13.9; Cleveland, 13.2; Chicago, 13. These F.B.I. figures indicate that jobs and power are not the only things on the rise in the Sun Belt.)

Cities, though, are much too dependent on everything and everybody working as one; when they grind to a halt, cities can be as dangerous as the most hateful small towns. During municipal strikes fires rage on, cops play poker, traffic idles (polluting the air even more than usual) and tons of garbage pile up to spoil the view and menace public health. The suspension of vital services has caused chaos in New Orleans, Memphis, San Antonio, New York and San Francisco. Strike negotiations invariably result in violence.

The following United Press story, dateline Philadelphia, illustrates the dangers of municipal maintenance:

> A woman was killed here yesterday when she was apparently swept into a city street-sweeping vehicle and crushed, police said. Authorities said the unidentified woman's body was ejected from the machine. A woman's purse and clothing were later found in the sweeper's trash storage bin, police said.

Power blackouts are more catastrophic in cities (they do not seem to incite looting in small towns), and contagious diseases scamper through dense populations with awful ease. Urbanites should even be more wary of commuters, who bring suburban neuroses to town. (*See* AIR, BOSTON, FLOOR-TO-CEILING WINDOWS, GARGOYLES, GARMENT DISTRICT, SUBURBS, SUBWAYS.)

CITIZEN'S ARREST

Citizen's arrest dates from medieval England and usually means more trouble for the tattletale than the accused. Taking the law into your own hands is foolish under any circumstances, and citizen's arrest is notorious. The vigilante can expect to be accosted, shot at, or sued.

COAL

Coal is our most abundant fossil fuel—bad news if there ever was. It lies beneath almost every state, with the heaviest deposits in the Midwest and Appalachia, and its inevitable extraction blights once-beautiful mountain regions and destroys lives and lifestyles. The burning of coal, having sulfates, nitrates, trace metals, and an array of carcinogenic organic compounds as by-products, may well darken skies and lungs forever. Clean air and good health are simply smudged out by the use of coal.

To get coal, the economical processes of strip mining blast away earth with dynamite, or tear it up in the 325-ton scoops of machines as tall as 20-story buildings. What's left is a treeless, desolate, deeply scarred landscape, an eyesore unfit for any ecological purpose. Equally violent aftereffects are most damaging in the mountainous areas, where the busy stripping activity sets up landslides, mudflows, and devastating erosion. Wastes left behind in slag heaps commonly contain sulphur oxides that poison water supplies and acidify rains. Cosmetic reclamation programs are a farce, for strip miners aren't about to do what is necessary to restore the ravaged earth to biological health. They'll opt instead for covering the stripped acreage with golf courses or other recreational facilities. (Strip mining is always dangerously expeditious; stripping for phosphate has practically ruined Polk County, Florida. To isolate one ton of phosphate requires converting 85,000 gallons of fresh water into slimy pools, and the naturally radioactive substance has seeped into homes. It's now blamed for a rash of lung cancer in western Florida.)

Deep mining of coal is kinder to land, but murder on miners. Mine explosions and black lung disease have long made coal mining, according to the National Safety Council, the most dangerous job in the private sector. A new scare is the industry's increased reliance on diesel-powered equipment, whose exhausts contain suspected carcinogens. When miners attempt to improve their lot, they face adversities as great as their working conditions; mining labor disputes have a history of violence, dating from the 1914 "Ludlow Massacre" at the Rockefeller mines in Colorado. Miners and their bosses are quick on the trigger.

So strip mining spoils land, and deep mining subverts health. However it is taken from the earth, the burning of coal produces some of the world's worst pollutants. (*See* AIR, WORKING.)

COFFEE

Balzac continually overcommitted himself to his publishers, so often drank coffee through the wee hours in order to meet his deadlines. Consequently, Balzac became a very unhealthy man.

Though it is a definite stimulus to late-night writing, coffee wreaks havoc in your body. Coffee contains twice as much caffeine as tea, and caffeine, which stimulates the central nervous system, is a poison. (There is little consolation for drinkers of decaffeinated coffee, for there is evidence that one of the chemicals used in the caffeine-removing process causes cancer.) The caffeine in a morning's cup of coffee can:

—accelerate heartbeat and respiration;
—increase secretions of hydrocholoric acid (causing heartburn) and adrenaline (which speeds up metabolism);
—stimulate the release of renin, a kidney enzyme linked to hypertension, and norepinephrine, the stress hormone;
—constrict blood vessels in the brain.

While caffeine may temporarily heighten concentration, it can't guarantee the quality of its addict's attention: When spiders were given caffeine in a test, they spun bizarrely asymmetrical webs.

36

If caffeine isn't scary enough, there are other reasons to fear coffee. Six carcinogenic pesticides, including Benzene Hexachloride (BHC) and the extremely toxic Malathion, have been isolated in beans imported from a dozen countries.

CORNFLAKES

Cornflakes can trigger a rare neurological disorder called myocolnus which prompts a severe asthmatic reaction and seizures, resulting in amnesia and paralysis.

They can also cause another kind of trouble altogether. As snowfall in *The Unholy Three,* a few bleached cornflakes reportedly lodged in Lon Chaney's throat, tearing his esophagus. Some bereaved fans swore that the actor's death was caused by the subsequent infection.

COSMETICS

Accidental poisoning by ingesting hair dye or astringent is one thing, but even used as directed, some cosmetics can cause disease, disorders, and death. Though skull-and-cross-bones ingredients such as chloroform, vinyl chloride, and mercury are now banned, cosmetic manufacturers have a long way to go to make their products safe. General Accounting, the congressional investigating office, issued a startling report in the summer of 1978 that detailed the connections between ordinary cosmetic products and cancer, birth defects, gastrointestinal disorders, skin and eye irritations, mental problems, respiratory conditions, hypertension, convulsions, headaches, and a multitude of infections, all because of sodium fluoride, boric acid, zinc chloride, coloring agents, and other harmful substances common to over-the-counter cosmetics.

The government study found toxic effects in about 600 common cosmetic ingredients, including 113 suspected of causing cancer, 12 known human carcinogens, 26 linked to birth defects, 20 that may wreck the nervous system, and 23 that irritate the skin, eyes, and mucous membranes.

The cosmetics involved are as various as their unbecoming side effects—even talcum powder can impact in the lungs, causing pulmonary diseases. The dangers of cosmetics may be obvious, such as hairsprays that are virtual blowtorches or shampoos that cause lesions; or they may effect subtle changes in the body's vital functions or alter behavior. There are 20 ingredients, for instance, that seem to bring on listlessness or other undesirable mental states.

Protection from the $9 billion-per-year industry will only be had with fundamental changes in the industrial conscience and the law. The federal Food, Drug and Cosmetic Act does not require manufacturers to file data on ingredients or cosmetic-related injuries, or test products for safety. Drugs included in cosmetic preparations are not subject to strict drug regulations, but the looser laws governing cosmetics. Cosmetics are treated with hardeners, softeners, dyes, perfumes, and preservatives, most of which exhibit side effects.

Adverse reactions are often experienced with the following products:

Bubble Baths

There's nothing so relaxing as a hot, frothy tub, nor so well liked: Annual U.S. sales of bubble bath products exceed $30,000,000. The bubble bursts, however, with the news that soaking in suds can strip away the body's protective oils, opening the skin to the baths' harsh soluble chemicals. Bubble baths are responsible for rashes, infections of the urinary tract and bladder, eye irritations, even respiratory problems and stomach disorders.

Eye Makeup

Wearing eye makeup is something that really can make you go blind. Mascara, liner, and shadow may harbor *Pseudomonas aeruginosa,* a bacterium that eats corneas. Minor abrasions—perhaps caused by contact lenses or makeup applicators—leave eyes wide open to the bacterial infection, which can cloud vision within 24 hours. One government survey of selected retail eye makeup found over 50 percent contaminated by the bacteria, and 10 percent containing various fungi. Routine use, involving fingers, saliva, and dirty swabs, assures the violation of any pure products. Makeup samples at display counters are of course especially germ-laden.

Contamination is hastened if preservatives aren't used in the preparations, but those chemicals—stearic acid, prophylene glycol, ceresin—may be more dangerous than the unadulterated product.

Hair Dye

Six chemicals in permanent hair dye appear to cause cancer in laboratory animals, and two of those ingredients are also used in a number of popular hair rinses and semi-permanent dyes. This, of course, means that blonds do not necessarily have more fun, and "punk" hair (those heads of luminescent red, pink, orange, purple, and green) is as frightening as its wearers want it to be.

Hairspray

The beehive was a hairdo of horrors, and it is comforting that the great stiff thing, so dependent on hairspray, has joined other extinct cones.

Blasted from explosive aerosol containers that are consumptive of ozone, most hairspray is flammable even hours after application.

Third-degree burns once crisped a woman who struck a match, at arm's length, after she'd lacquered her hair. Another woman died when her cigarette ignited the hairspray that had dried on her hair and clothes. Similar things have happened with spray colognes and deodorants.

CREDIT BUREAUS

Credit bureaus know too much about the 112,000,000 people who carry credit cards, and anyone else who has applied for loans, signed leases, or filed for insurance. People are denied credit by various institutions because of bureau reports that may be impertinent, punitive, out-of-date, or based on information that is simply false. Responsible consumers are punished by credit bureaus for being single, old, sick, female, new in town, or sexually promiscuous. To get the goods on you, credit agents employ, among other things, the highly scientific process of soliciting neighbors' opinions.

Clearing your record requires documentation in person of your alleged financial misbehavior, a complicated process that involves absence from work and risking traffic, headaches, and ulcers.

No matter how erroneous they may be, bad credit reports mean that you may have to do without a few basics to survival, such as smoke alarms, microwave and x-ray shields, gas masks, and bomb shelters.

CYANOCRYLATE ADHESIVES

"Super glues," developed in the 1950s, create a bond that can be stronger than human skin and muscle, so a spot of misplaced glue could fuse fingers or worse. Among the most notorious are the toxic cyano-crylate adhesives, which are sometimes used to close surgical incisions and have been linked to chromosome breakage and subsequent birth defects.

D

DIETS

Be suspicious of diets that promise rapid weight loss while depriving you of essential energy sources. Losing weight is hard work, so you can distrust any program claiming pounds will "melt away" while you just sit there. Diets can be cultish (The Zen Macrobiotic Diet), glamorous (The Drinking Man's Diet), and dumb (The Ice Cream Diet). They can also be dangerous.

One out of three Americans is overweight, including about 15 percent of the teenaged population. No wonder: The average national diet contains 43 percent fat, and each of us ingests over 1,000 pounds of sugar per year. Some have gotten rich off our fat. The diet industry grosses about $10 billion annually in dietetic foods, fat doctor bills, health spas, appetite killers, exercise devices, and various reducing preparations. Weight Watchers, Inc. grosses over $20 million each year. Diet books promising a slim new you are surpassed in sales only by dictionaries and Bibles.

Though experts continue to debate the good and bad of cholesterol, vitamins, and calorie counting, they do agree, to no one's surprise, that too much food—especially the low-protein, high-sugar variety that fills the stomach while falling far short of nutritional needs—is bad. It would be unfair to say that all diets are impractical; except for the most exotic and extreme, they stress low-carbohydrate, high-protein eating, encouraging plenty of vegetables, fluids, and small portions of lean meat. The most serious charge that can be leveled at these diets is that they are unoriginal, since they are slight variations on a diet developed in 1863 by a British surgeon, Dr. William Harvey, for his overweight patients.

Some physicians have made fortunes prescribing appetite suppressants, such as amphetamines, which are probably more dangerous than obesity. Commonly known as speed, their regular consumption will keep you buzzing day and night, give you heart palpitations, and a habit.

Dr. Robert Atkins' famous diet took the low-carbohydrate plan to an extreme, championing a near-elimination of carbohydrates. A few months after its publication, the Atkins diet was under fire from doctors and concerned individuals. The American Medical Association's Council on Food and Nutrition condemned it, and issued a specific warning about carbohydrate deprivation. When the body suddenly loses carbohydrates, it produces ketones, which compete with urea to get to the kidneys for excretion. The ketones usually win out, and the accumulation of uric acid causes gout and kidney stones. (Ketones are also exhaled, causing bad breath, the very least of your problems.) Atkins' diet allows its followers large quantities of saturated fats and cholesterol, which you should also be afraid of, since they contribute to arteriosclerosis.

The most controversial diet in recent history is the liquid protein diet, which allots a mere 300 calories per day to its believers. Liquid protein is derived from a gelatin of animal hides, tendons, and bones.

An osteopath, Dr. Robert Linn, has commercialized the liquid protein diet in a book. His instructions amount to little more than a fast, and consist of drinking eight ounces of the animal extract each day, lots of water, and taking vitamin and mineral supplements. During a total fast, the body burns stored fat and protein—it simply begins to digest itself. Dr. Linn's diet keeps that from happening, but it overlooks other nutritional needs, chiefly our full mineral demands and blood pressure requirements.

Liquid protein is available over-the-counter, and some have taken to it as if it were a magic potion, ignoring the label that suggests medical supervision. At last count, twelve people have dieted to death on liquid protein. (*See* FASTING, YOGURT.)

DIGITAL TIMEPIECES

Clocks and watches are losing their handsome faces to a technology that contributes to societal stress: No one needs to know that it's 3:23 or 7:19. Time is all the more anxiety-producing with the obnoxious precision of the computer-based digital devices, which are making obsolete generations of people who can tell time.

DISTRICT OF COLUMBIA

I will not belabor the dangers of bungling bureaucrats, the Pentagon or the I.R.S., but will confine this entry to the capital's grim 27 percent homicide rate. Washington's rate is far greater than the national average and is 11 points above Louisiana's, the state with the highest rate of murders-per-100,000 people.

DOCTORS

> I often say that a great doctor kills more people than a great general. —*Baron Gottfried Wilhelm von Leibnitz*

Doctors overexpose patients to x-rays. Doctors may continue to practice no matter how incompetent they become. Doctors have been convicted of sexually molesting patients and dispensing illicit drugs. Doctors have secrets and don't tell on each other. Doctors remove uteruses and tonsils like it's going out of style (and it is). But there's hope: Medical school enrollments are down.

There are about 400,000 doctors in the United States, and though Ralph Nader's Health Research Group says that 25 percent of them are unfit to prescribe drugs, it's hard to get out of a doctor's office without an expensive remedy or two for what ails you. Mal-doctors are absolutely responsible for the widescale use of depressants that deliver a variety of blows to the central nervous system. One of these, a benzodiazepine called Valium, is the most prescribed drug in America, and produces severe withdrawal symptoms. Seconal and Nembutal, powerful barbiturates that block the body's vital neurological signals, are prescribed with near-abandon, as are antibiotics, the great cure-alls that cause anemia. These and other drugs may provoke allergic reactions, but tests are seldom administered—there's no way to do that over the telephone, which is as close as some doctors get to their patients today.

In malpractice trials, doctors have been held responsible for many operating-room tragedies: misreading x-rays and removing healthy organs, leaving surgical tools inside patients, overdoing anesthesia. Perhaps more frightening is the way doctors endanger patients by performing unnecessary surgery. *The New York Times* reported that 260,000 of 1975's 787,000 hysterectomies shouldn't have happened, and that nearly two-thirds of the year's tonsillectomies were absolutely needless. In all, 12,000 deaths resulted that year from non-essential operations, some of them performed by doctors who were drunk, drugged, or professionally unqualified. Doctors have now protected themselves with malpractice insurance, whose exorbitant costs are passed on to patients.

Most professionals with life and death in their hands—pilots, for instance—must prove their competence annually, but doctors never have to face any sort of license renewal. (*See* ANESTHESIA, APPENDECTOMIES, ASPIRIN, DIETS, FOOD AND DRUG INTERACTIONS, INTESTINAL BYPASS SURGERY, ORTHOPEDICS, PRE-SURGICAL SHAVING, RADIOPHARMACEUTICALS, X-RAYS.)

DOGS

In a national poll, Americans have said that one of their chief concerns is dogs and their waste. The fear is warranted. There are about 500 dogs per square mile in the United States, and each is capable of transmitting 65 diseases to humans, including one that causes blindness. Children actually suffer more from dog bites than all other diseases combined. And when dogs attack kids, they usually go for the face.

DOUBLE-Y MUTANTS

Female sex cells have X chromosomes; male, X and Y. If the male's X is used in conception, the result will be an XX zygote, which will produce a girl; if his Y is used, a boy, XY, is conceived. In rare cases, two Y chromosomes may be united, making an XYY male.

If you buy the notion of male aggressiveness, the XYY syndrome can be seen as a double dose of that. XYY men tend to be tall, blond, strong, and violent. That such mutants have been convicted of brutal crimes (Richard Speck is one) lends credence to the theory.

DUMB CANE

This is a dieffenbachia, very big these days in hotel lobbies and restaurants. It was also popular with South American Indians who used its juices to make poison arrows.

Every green inch of dumb cane is poisonous, and it shares with water hemlock an extraordinary effect: striking victims mute. (Johann Friedrich Dieffenbach, a nineteenth-century Prussian surgeon who advocated severing the tongues of stutterers, was also, appropriately enough, the part-time botanist who identified and gave his name to this plant, the poison of which paralyzes the speech organs.) Bare contact with the mouth can cause the larynx and pharynx to blister and swell, blocking speech. Death by suffocation may occur with a great deal of swelling and—how awful—the victim wouldn't be able to call for help.

E

EAR-PIERCING

Ear-piercing leads to infections, the unsurprising result of undergoing this minor surgery in jewelry stores or at home. The metal alloys in earrings then worsen things by inflaming the jabbed lobes.

THE EAST SOUTH CENTRAL STATES

Year after dreaded year, the news is the same for the area encompassing Kentucky, Tennessee, Alabama, and Mississippi: The East South Central death rate is the nation's highest. Blame it on poor highways, coal mines and inadequate medical care.

EATING SNOW

Snow is likely to contain sulfate and nitrate pollutants, which means that snow ice cream, one of the original natural treats, can now cause asthma, chronic bronchitis, emphysema, eye and skin irritation, and cardiovascular diseases. Snow, especially in congested cities, contains known human carcinogens, picked up from the organic poisons of fossil-fuel combustion. (*See* AIR.)

ENCOUNTER GROUPS

> You gain strength, courage and confidence by every experience in
> which you really stop to look fear in the face.
>
> —*Eleanor Roosevelt*

Over 20 million Americans—for the most part, bored middle-class
whites—have encountered encounter groups, those explosive combinations of gestalt therapy, confession, basic training, meditation, and
performance. The idea is to get in touch with yourself via a series of
humiliations, strikes, and strokes. Caution and discretion are thrown to
the wind. Psyches are ruptured.

The charlatans who run the various self-help institutions cash in on
the vulnerabilities of profoundly lonely people, and have convinced
some "progressive" employers to enroll their employees in training and
motivation sessions.

What people get from encounter groups are invasions of privacy,
physical injuries (from trusting others to throw them about in order to
force relaxation), and, in some cases, nervous breakdowns, shattered
morales, and acute psychoses.

Sensitivity isn't something that can be taught during a weekend
retreat.

ESCALATORS

Escalators are dangerous for the simple reason that their malfunction
would not be catastrophic. Unaccompanied by any sort of crash or
explosion, the moving stairway would just become eerily stationary, an
unheralded disaster. Imagine an escalator stalled in a department store,
panicked shoppers groping their way to safety.

F

FAMILY AND FRIENDS

The Old Testament and Sophocles made it famous, and intra-family violence, if you read the tabloids at all, now seems to be all the rage. About 19 percent of murderers and their victims are (were) related to one another, and 40 percent are at least acquainted. This makes for sensational stories: ANNIVERSARY CELEBRATION BLOODY; I WAS RAPED BY MY NEIGHBOR; SLAIN BY TWIN; and the Rupert Murdoch classic, UNCLE TORTURES TOT WITH HOT FORK.

Avoid family reunions, and don't make friends. (*See* CAINISM.)

FASTING

The two chief reasons people have fasted—to assuage the gods, and to effect political change—are stupid. The only thing accomplished rather quickly by those who fast is the supine position. Deprived of regular deliveries, the body tries to find food within, so begins digesting itself. Only the enormously fat can afford that. In little time, fasting produces bad breath, hallucinations, irritability, self-absorption, and insensitivity to stimuli such as fire alarms, gale warnings, jumps in the Richter scale, and the growling of wild animals.

FIREWORKS

Americans rediscovered fireworks during the Bicentennial and the pyrotechnics business is booming once again: Sales of firecrackers and other things that go bang in the night top $100 million during Fourth of July celebrations. It'd be nice to sit back and watch the fancier ones light up the sky, but no one can afford to do that because the spectacle is dangerous. About 9 million people are burned or blinded by fireworks every year.

The legal trade of fireworks is bound by new government regulations on powder content, fusing, and labeling, but more and more of what's sold are illicit explosives from the People's Republic, Taiwan, and Japan. These imports are staggeringly high-powered, yet are sold on the street, packed with powder and short on fuse. One item, the "blockbuster," is as strong as a quarter-stick of dynamite and can demolish a room. When shipments are seized, the army is called in because police bomb squads are afraid to touch them.

Besides their ability to send eyes and hands flying, fireworks and their adolescent consumers are also big starters of fires in abandoned buildings, open fields, and parks.

FLOOR-TO-CEILING WINDOWS

The point of stories about blazing skyscrapers is that much of the new architecture greatly enhances one's chances of perishing in a high-rise fire. Probably more than any other feature, immobile floor-to-ceiling windows make this so, since they cannot be opened to let smoke out or firefighters in.

Elevators in these buildings also inhibit survival, for most are equipped with heat-sensitive controls that force them to open onto the floors where flames are raging.

FLORIDA

Florida, that precariously dangling peninsula, attracts reckless vacationers, depressing retirees, and thunderstorms. (*See* RETIREMENT, LIGHTNING.)

To be sure, some of the natives are having fun: The state reports the nation's highest incidence of syphilis. And, not surprisingly, skin cancer is epidemic in Florida. (*See* THE SUN.)

Escapees from zoos, abandoned exotic pets, and stowaways on tropical trade vessels—encouraged by the state's mild climate and network of waterways—account for Florida's exploding population of strange species. Among the more unpleasant aliens: alligators, piranhas, poisonous toads, wild cats, disease-carrying snails, and pythons. (*See* SNAILS.)

FLYING

Turkish Airlines is not the most dangerous in the world,* but no other carrier has so conclusively demonstrated how wrong flying is. Most crashes occur at takeoff and landing, when speed and altitude are low enough to perhaps spare some lives. But not the Turkish Airlines DC–10 that crashed outside of Paris on March 10, 1974: The 300-ton jet fell 12,000 feet, smashing into the ground at 500 miles per hour, obliterating itself and the 346 people on board.

Just about everybody flies today (a half billion passengers annually on international flights alone) and a well-publicized percentage of all air travelers are fretting about the big crash. What they don't realize is that there are other things to worry about, such as jet lag, the disruption of the body's circadian cycle. Caused by crossing time zones, jet lag does more than wear you down: It can actually make you sick. X-rays that examine carry-on luggage and the devices that electronically frisk your person are cause for alarm, as is the radiation from microwave ovens used to prepare malnourishing in-flight meals. Non-smoking passengers should also be wary of the cigarette smoke that inevitably wafts over into

*Destination Disaster, by Paul Eddy, Elaine Potter and Bruce Page (New York: Quadrangle, 1976) investigated flying safety in general and the Turkish Airlines crash specifically. According to the authors' survey, the ten airlines with the worst crash records are ALIA (Royal Jordanian), VIASA (Venezuela), Egyptair, TAROM (Romanian), Turkish Airlines, Middle East Airlines, Nigeria, AVIACO (Spain), Air India, and Philippine Airlines.

their section, while asking why smokers, who obviously aren't keen on staying alive, get to sit in the rear of the cabin, where one is more likely to survive a crash. Hijackers and their bombs, guns, and abrasive behavior should also be on the hazard list.

The Concorde

Supersonic transport has nothing to recommend it, except the feature of less time in the air. The Concorde, which shouldn't have left its hangar, is so noisy that its pilots have to execute a hair-raising maneuver that risks a runway somersault. Upon takeoff—the most dangerous moment of flight—the pilots tilt the supersonic plane at a 25° angle, practically scraping a wingtip on the runway. Traffic controllers at Kennedy Airport have told the *New York Post* that the sudden dip leaves no more than 70 feet between the ground and the jet, and, what's more, the stunt keeps the pilots in such a frenzy that they can't respond to commands from the tower.

Landing—the next most crucial time in flight—the Concorde once again causes great worry, since it lacks the nimbleness to suddenly switch runways, or in any way delay its approach. Other craft have to get out of Concorde's way.

In between takeoff and landing, of course, the Concorde's exhausts of nitrogen oxide are destroying stratospheric ozone.

Harry S. Truman Airport/Charlotte Amalie

Pilots give the infamous Black Star to Harry S. Truman Airport at Charlotte Amalie on St. Thomas. (The Virgin Island airport shares the "critically deficient" rating with Los Angeles International, where, because of noise regulations, pilots are required to approach from the Pacific, often necessitating steep turns, long holding patterns, and battles with air currents.) When an American Airlines Boeing 727 crashed at Charlotte Amalie on April 27, 1976, killing 37, it was HST Airport's third major disaster in ten years. What's the jinx? For one thing, the runway isn't long enough—at 4,658 feet, it barely meets federal standards. The airport is also surrounded by mountain ranges on two sides, hills at one end, and the Caribbean at the other. Thick fog is abundant. Nothing larger than a 727 is allowed to land there until some changes are made. Among the drastic suggestions are extending the runway into the sea and slicing off the tops of the mountains.

St. Thomas is a popular island, a big vacation spot and convention site. Bluebeard's and Blackbeard's castles are there, but it's the airport that should give tourists the jitters.

Helicopters

A flying machine based on a rotating wing wasn't one of Leonardo da Vinci's better ideas. Don't envy the fellow who zips off to a business meeting in a helicopter, for there's a good chance he'll not meet his stockbrokers.

Helicopters are inherently unstable contraptions, contending as their blades must with the constant opposition of lift and drag. Airflow and the likelihood of staying aloft are reduced when helicopters hover or fly at low speeds, tricks that whirlybird pilots are frequently called upon to perform. During 1969 and 1970, 1,200 people died in 2,300 helicopter crashes. The odds get worse as their demand increases—in military and emergency service, news gathering, industrial transports, and as taxis.

Helicopters are usually flown at low altitudes, so quite easily slam into hillsides and skyscrapers, and have even tripped over utility lines. That low altitude, however, does not make for an inconsequential fall: Helicopters are very heavy and crash with immense, fiery impact. The multi-ton, charred wreckage is awful—it's a wonder there are ever any survivors, especially when you consider that the altitude thwarts escape via parachute.

Riding a helicopter is an alien experience for most people, and decapitation has been the grisly result of boarding a chopper too late, or deboarding one too soon.

(*See* BALLOONING, HANG GLIDING, SKYDIVING.)

THE FOOD CHAIN

If it weren't for the food chain, we might stand a fighting chance against the chemicals dumped in oceans and sprayed on fields. But the food chain is one in which we are hopelessly bound, it links the transfer of energy from organism to organism, from plankton to people. But energy isn't the only thing passed up the evolutionary line. All sorts of poisons ascend the food chain, and in increasingly concentrated form: It is not unusual for toxicants in grain to concentrate a thousand times in the flesh of livestock. So it doesn't matter that you're unlikely to directly consume pesticides; thanks to the food chain, they'll get back to you, and in slugger doses. What the food chain means, and why it's such a cruel aspect of nature, is that the very thing on which we depend for energy and nutrition is also our doom. (*See* BUGS, POLYCHLORINATED BIPHENYLS.)

THE FOOD AND DRUG ADMINISTRATION

The FDA is there to protect the public health, to keep food and drug industries in the business of producing and selling clean and safe products, so it's the one bureaucracy whose slow-motion is particularly frightening. Food and drug producers don't want food and drugs to do what comes naturally, and the FDA allows them chemicals to assist that end—dyes; emulsifiers; stabilizers; flavor enhancers; bleaching and maturing agents; sequestrants; humectants; anticaking, firming, foaming, clarifying, and curing agents. The FDA is quick to approve an array of additives, but very slow to ban them. (It took the FDA years to ban Red 2, even with hard evidence that the dye causes cancer.)

Its critics charge that the agency actually endorses the use of additives, and lacks the commitment or motivation to make food companies obey new laws. Labeling regulations, while improved, are still fraught with inconsistencies and hide possible dangers: The FDA should force food producers to detail such things as "artificial flavors."

If you think the FDA is your friend, you ought to study the agency's "Filth Guidelines." The FDA *allows* 12 insect heads in 100 grams of fig paste and 3 rodent hairs in 100 grams of apple butter; 9.9 percent of any shipment of coffee beans may contain cockroach legs, grasshopper wings, or other insect parts. (What can you expect, though, from the FDA labs, which are so decrepit and dirty that they don't even meet the standards of the Occupational Safety and Health Administration?)

The FDA okays additives that cause allergies, birth defects, miscarriages, and various diseases. Used as a preservative, benzoic acid interferes with growth and has caused neurological disorders. A sequestrant, calcium disodium-EDTA, damages human kidneys. Ammoniated glycyrrhizin is related to heart failure and hypertension in men and women, and brominated vegetable oils seem to affect every single organ in laboratory animals. Each has won FDA approval. A House subcommittee may have uncovered a reason for this permission of poisons: Several FDA officials have financial interests in some of the food companies they are responsible for regulating. (See RED FOOD.)

FOOD AND DRUG INTERACTIONS

It shouldn't be a surprise that such generally dangerous substances as food and drugs would chemically collude to bring you to your knees. Food and drugs are a powerful duo, and doctors and pharmaceutical companies are disserving the public by not giving more explicit directions regarding the mixing of medications with certain meals and beverages.

Carbonated drinks and citric juices, for example, dissolve drugs before they get to the small intestine, where they would be more effectively absorbed. Other liquids also thwart that process, or even render medications useless or dangerous. Some combinations are fatal.

The calcium in dairy products makes tetracycline about as effective as a sugar pill. Blood-clotting vitamin K (found in liver and leafy vegetables) can interfere with anticoagulant drugs. One of the most dangerous combinations is monoamine oxidase (MAO) inhibitors with aged and fermented foods, such as cheese, salami, yogurt, liver, canned figs, bananas, soy sauce, beer, and sherry. MAO inhibitors are prescribed for high blood pressure and depression, so their consumption with those tyramine-containing foods may result in a drastic rise in blood pressure that can cause headaches, brain hemorrhage, and even death.

Alcohol, a drug itself, should of course never be used to wash down medicine, not even aspirin tablets.

FORD

Ford's ideas aren't always better. In fact, the ones the motor company has had for fuel tanks, automatic transmissions, and emission controls have turned out to be real bombs, leading to 21 separate recalls in the first half of 1978, for a total of 5.5 million cars and trucks.

Five years' worth of automobiles (1971–1976 Pintos and 1975–1976 Bobcats) had their fuel tanks positioned mere inches from the rear bumpers, so that even a 30-mph impact could send an exploded tank into the passenger compartments. Thanks to investigations by *Mother Jones,* Ford recalled, reluctantly, over 1.5 million Pintos and 30,000 Bobcats, and was forced to pay enormous damages for burns and deaths related to the cars' irresponsible design. Although preliminary road tests demonstrated the likelihood of the fuel-tank disasters, the cars were approved for production.

Between 1970 and 1978, Ford produced cars and light trucks in which the automatic transmissions had a tendency to jump from park to reverse. The National Highway Traffic Safety Administration warned that there could be 14,000,000 of the self-willed vehicles on the road, their literally "automatic" transmissions capable of switching gears while the cars idle. Leaping backwards without warning, the cars have crushed people against buildings.

Ford's feeble efforts to keep the air cleaner have been thwarted by emission-control devices in 1978 models that become disengaged and release gasoline fumes. The defect afflicts 1,475,000 cars and trucks—over half of the company's output that year.

FRANCE

France leads all other nations in per capita consumption of wine and spirits, at a rate three times that of America. Forty percent of France's fatal traffic accidents are the fault of drunken drivers. Turn back to ALCOHOL.

FRATERNITIES

The irrationality of ritual, mob behavior, and the identity confusion attendant to group membership all come together in fraternities, those clubs that provide security and a sense of belonging to men who would never admit to needing such.

Fraternity members reserve their most passionate feelings about parades and parties, and get riled over the athletic and academic successes of their rival organizations. They live a considerable distance from the real world in their chapter houses, which are veritable forts from which obscenities and empty liquor bottles fly.

Fraternities are dangerous to their own members because of the sadomasochistic activity that bonds and occasionally kills them. Outlawed but rampant, hazing usually begins with verbal abuse and the insertion of foreign objects into body orifices, then moves on to heavy stuff. During an initiation in 1976, one student at Queens College was accidentally stabbed to death by his fellow pledges; others have died after being forced to "chugalug" straight alcohol. Fraternity boys are eager to prove their allegiance, and have submitted to electrocution, live burial, fasting, branding irons, and wallowing in filth.

Mexican jails are probably safer than fraternity houses.

THE FULL MOON

It's not been cited in court as grounds for acquittal, but there does seem to be a link between the full moon and the incidence of passionate crime. Selective data show that a given month's homicides do peak at full moon; further study may show this to be more broadly true. Some have speculated that human passions wax and wane with the moon, not a terribly farfetched extension of biophysical forces. But it could be much simpler than that: The full moon allows murderers a better view of their victims.

G

GAMBLING

Gambling attracts hordes of people, who attract larcenists and even murderers. Atlantic City's street crime jumped 25 percent after the opening of the Boardwalk casinos. But gamblers may be their own worst enemies—see NEVADA.

GARGOYLES

A lot of horrors date from the Middle Ages: the public flogging and maiming of criminals, feudalism, the Black Death, and gargoyles.

Modern architects think they're being nostalgic or artistic when they decorate buildings with the gothic uglies, but they're only being negligent. Originally designed as waterspouts, the once-gurgling gargoyles are now purely ornamental, unattached to a superstructure, and vulnerable to the corrosive elements of polluted cities. It's only a matter of time before the grotesque statuary hits the street. Gargoyles are on the verge of tumbling down—that's why steel aprons are cantilevered around some older buildings.

THE GARMENT DISTRICT

It's hard to imagine an area more crowded with people, cars, and trucks, and possessing such a potential for mishaps than New York City's Garment District, between 6th and 8th Avenues and 34th and 40th Streets. The people probably won't hurt you intentionally, but all those racks of clothes thrown about have knocked down pedestrians and caused wrecks. There are also a lot of falling objects there. A well-known case concerns a young man whose head caught a yard-long brass curtain rod end-on, so that it protruded from the top of his head and his mouth. Once the rod was extracted, the man only suffered a headache—amazing, since it had bisected his brain. The Garment District should be made a hard-hat area.

GENETIC ENGINEERING

The miniest of computers, deoxyribonucleic acid (DNA) is the constituent of chromosomes that determines exactly what an organism will be. Genetic engineering involves splicing threads of DNA from one creature to another, like so much film, and it could result in some real-life horror movies indeed. Even advocates of recombinant DNA conceded the possibility of creating unstoppable horrors—a ghastly critter with, say, the coat of a porcupine, the fangs of a cobra, and the nimble body of a parakeet. But the result is likely to be more insidious: indestructible, ravaging bacteria that could wipe out entire civilizations.

Scientists have never been overly burdened with accountability, even to a public that funds their research, and this autonomy is nowhere more consequential than in genetic engineering, the willy-nilly rearrangement of chromosomal structures that effectively bypasses millions of years of evolution.

Genetic engineering is conducted in labs around the world, so there is no telling where the first super-molecular menace will emerge.

GIRAFFES

Giraffes have everything going for them: They're giant (about 18 feet tall); fast (30 miles per hours); possess keen sight, smell, and hearing; and with a mean kick, their front hooves could deftly slice off the top of your head.

GIRDLES

Girdles cause varicose veins by choking circulation to the legs.

"GLOOMY SUNDAY"

This song is more dangerous than the Sirens'. The original Hungarian version, "Szomoru Vasárnap," was written in 1933 and a number of Europeans were actually swayed by its suggestion. Paul Robeson introduced Sam M. Lewis' translation of "Gloomy Sunday" in 1936, but it was Billie Holiday's 1941 rendition that allegedly drove American audiences to suicide.

The lament's composer, Rezso Seress (a citizen of Hungary, whose suicide rate is the world's highest), killed himself in 1968.

GOLDEN GATE BRIDGE

Along the entire west coast of North America, the greatest amplitudes of tsunamis have been recorded near the Golden Gate Bridge (*see* TECTONICS). In addition to its geological grimness, the great suspension seems to lure suicides. So many people have jumped off the Golden Gate that some San Franciscans have proposed that a pad and pen be left at its peak to facilitate suicide notes. Since it opened in 1937, 1.4 people *per month* have jumped from the bridge.

GOLF

Even golf. Doctors are finding lots of injuries associated with the mannered game of the doubleknit set. Golfers have been treated for inflamed tendons, bursitis, nerve damage, elbow and wrist strains, ruptured underarm blood vessels, and even a few small broken bones. But lower back problems are by far the most common golf-related injuries.

Back pain is the unsurprising consequence of standing erect and thrashing at a golf ball; a hundred miles per hour is the average swing's speed. If amateur golfers would relax on the course, they'd encounter less wrenching pain; instead, they swing as fiercely as the pros they see on television. The pros' tightly coiled swing emphasizes an extreme upper body windup with little rotation of the hips, and it isn't something weekend golfers should try since it overextends every joint in the body, and puts great pressure on the spine. As it is now, most golfers balk at the demands of such playing; their bodies simply give out mid-swing. The result is probably a sand-trapped ball, but that beats a slipped disc.

H

HAIR IMPLANTS

The rejection phenomenon that plagues major organ transplants is at work in the hair implant, whereby a thin artificial scalp, into which hair has been woven, is actually sewn onto a bald person's head. Sutures invariably fester, and blood may have a hard time getting under the rug, a condition that can cause cerebral damage. The implant is also difficult to clean, and usually begins to smell and even attract lice and maggots.

Hair transplants are more akin to skin grafts, are more painful and expensive than implants, but they're more effective, too. You ought to think twice, however, about having holes bored into the head's subcutaneous tissues—one slip, and you've got a punctured brain rather than a relocated plug of hair—or maybe a hirsute cerebrum.

Hair implants and transplants for destitute scalps are further evidence that vanity is a dangerous state of mind.

HANDGUNS

Don't let anyone tell you differently: Handguns are used to kill people and they are legally had by practically any adult in 44 states. Fully one-half of all murder victims are blown away by handguns.

HANG GLIDING

"Oh God," said Lord Byron, "it is a fearful thing to see the human soul take wing." Maybe so, but in the case of hang gliding it is also spectacularly beautiful. Hang gliders have come to closest of all glider pilots to actually experience the pterodactyl's prehistoric flight. Some aeronautical engineers are wary of the ultralight aircraft, and say they are unstable contraptions, as worthless as matchsticks against the force of the wind. Still, there are over 8,000 hang-gliding enthusiasts around the world, soaring from rocky cliffs in NASA-designed gliders.

Slung into multi-colored nylon wings, hang gliders are surely the most glorious daredevils around. Once they've donned their Icarus get-up, hang gliders jump headlong into the wind and swirl around for as long as thirty minutes. A hang glider crashes about once a month, but the real danger of the sport may be for us bird-watchers. In national parks, popular hang-gliding areas, most glider-related accidents and fatalities occur when awed spectators tumble from observation ledges. (*See* BALLOONING, FLYING, SKYDIVING.)

HEIGHT

Acrophobia is irrational: Heights can't possibly hurt you, but height, as in tallness, can. A study bears it out: People who stand less than five feet-nine inches live longer than taller folks.

HETEROSEXUALS

The headlines might have you believe otherwise, but sex crimes—pedophilia, lewdness, and, of course, rape—are overwhelmingly heterosexual in nature. To be frank, everything you've heard about dirty old men is true. Many studies of sexual criminality, including a 1969 report by the American Humane Association, indicate that 90 to 91 percent of all child molestations are committed by older men against minor-age girls.

HICCUPS

You could hiccup to death. When the diaphragm convulses and the glottis arbitrarily snaps shut, both resulting from phrenic nervousness, hiccups are disrupting your life. The diaphragm, more than any other, is the breathing muscle, and it is important that its contractions be regular, its behavior calm.

Plato wrote about hiccups, and their causes and cures haven't changed much since 347 B.C. Hiccups are brought on by jabbering while scarfing down meals, hooting, excessive smoking, emotional stress, or speedy ingestion of hot or cold drinks. Hiccups frequently announce indigestion, follow surgery, or accompany various ills, from appendicitis to brain tumors. Age-old cures of holding breath, trickling water down the throat, and being booed are really about as effective as newer practices of hypnosis, controlled inhalation of carbon dioxide, and the prescription of strong suppressant drugs. Only severing the spinal phrenic nerve guarantees cessation of hiccups, but that procedure could have a depressing effect on the entire respiratory apparatus.

Unless they're soon squelched, hiccups can lead to insomnia, suffocation, fatal exhaustion, and dread.

HIGHWAYS

In descending order, the fatality rates for motor vehicle accidents are highest on the horrible highways of New Mexico, Wyoming, Nevada, Vermont, Arizona, Montana, West Virginia, Louisiana, Alaska, and Idaho.

Also be wary of motoring in the thirteen states where traffic laws are deemed obsolete and noncompliant by the National Highway Safety Council:

—Maine
—Massachusetts
—Connecticut
—Rhode Island
—New Jersey
—Virginia
—North Carolina
—Alabama
—Mississippi

—Missouri
—Iowa
—Wisconsin
—Michigan

HITCHHIKING

There's little good to be said about cars and highways and traveling, and all that bad news comes together in hitchhiking, a free ride that is often a pedestrian's last.

Police records from various locales show that up to 70 percent of a year's rape victims had been hitchhiking at the time of their abduction. It's not always been this way—drivers used to be the losers in the relationship.

Like other things, hitchhiking is especially dangerous in Uganda, where thumbers report they have to dodge gunfire.

Hitchhikers are easy targets. Take a bus.

HOME

When presented with an opportunity to leave the house, don't hesitate. Get going—for an hour or a season. You'll be much safer out of the house:

- —away from family and friends who, as we've seen, are more likely to kill you than total strangers;
- —away from the liquor cabinet; alcoholics are made not in bars, but at home;
- —away from the 15 (of 250,000 on the market) dangerous household products found in most homes; if their ingredients don't get you, the explosive aerosol containers will;
- —away from flora, the green menace that has made apartments and houses lush but lethal (English ivy, lantana, larkspur, dieffen-

bachia, elephant ears, wisteria and yucca are a few of the hundreds
of poisonous plants people decorate their living quarters with);
—away from the radiation machines that can twist chromosomes and
cause blindness: microwave ovens, automatic door-openers,
high-powered radios, color television sets;
—away from snakes, which are more likely to bite people before
they've wandered far from their houses;
—and away from these "most dangerous" items on the Consumer
Product Safety Commission's hazard list:

1. stairs
2. bicycles
3. nails and tacks
4. glass doors, windows and mirrors
5. end tables
6. rocking chairs
7. playground equipment
8. lawn mowers
9. knives
10. floors and flooring materials
11. chain link fences
12. bleaches, dyes, cleaning agents
13. liquid fuels
14. swimming pools
15. bathtubs and showers

Bathrooms

Until they reach middle age, Americans are more likely to be done in by
accidents than any other cause. Two-thirds of all accidents, fatal or not,
occur at home. Though one must reckon with kitchens' various heat-
producing appliances, bathrooms constitute the more formidable
domestic territory. These chambers of hygienic pursuit and primping are
rigged for broken bones, burns, gashes, electrocutions, and drownings.
It's a wonder anyone ever makes it out alive.

Consider an average bathroom's inventory: flammable and/or toxic cosmetics and cleansers, many in explosive aerosol containers; razor blades; dozens of prescription and over-the-counter drugs; electrical gadgets. And its equipment: plumbing that disgorges gallons of scalding water; mirrors and glass doors, which rank fourth on the Consumer Hazard List; slippery tile and linoleum; bathtubs and shower stalls, the cause of about 200,000 injuries each year that require hospital treatment. When people fall in tubs and showers (sometimes by trusting poorly-mounted towel racks and soap dishes for support) glass doors are there to sliver their fractured bodies. If they're knocked unconscious, they may drown in an inch of water. Errant radios, hair dryers, sunlamps, and electric razors could make for your last bath.

And bathroom doors lock, a feature that certainly complicates rescue efforts, and may explain the allure of bathrooms to suicides.

HOUSTON COPS

By many standards, Houston's are the worst cops in the nation: They're disorganized, corrupt, poorly trained, and, most pertinent to your fears, overarmed and brutal. It's said that only Philadelphia's force comes close to matching Houston's arrogant officers, whose pistol-wielding "law enforcement" has made international news.

Often working in small armies, Houston police have battered suspects and violated the basic rights of citizens, law-abiding or not. Sixteen of them once burst into a hotel room to gun down a man suspected of a misdemeanor drug offense. Critics have cited as part of the problem the department's tradition of self-rule: For years, its chiefs have proudly declined funds (and interference) from the feds, and have never been keen on setting up a division of internal affairs.

The local judiciary, in the rare instances of police indictment, is easy on the virtually all-white HPD, letting the cops off with minimal punishment, if any at all. Three of them got one year for "violating the civil rights" of a Mexican-American man who was beaten and drowned in their custody.

A few brave Houstonians have organized People to Fight Brutality; so far, none of its members have turned up at the bottom of the city's bayou.

HUNGARY

Only the relentlessly cheerful should live in Hungary—its suicide rate is the world's highest, with 40 such deaths per 100,000 people. Denmark, Austria, and Finland follow with 23. The U.S. rate is 13.3 per 100,000. (*See* NEVADA.)

HURRICANES

Beginning life as "depressions" over tropical waters during summer and fall, hurricanes become hurricanes once their winds have whipped up at 75 mph. Don't feel safe just because you may not live on the Gulf Coast: Hurricanes have blown from the Florida Keys to New England, from Galveston to the Plains.

A hurricane's size (400 miles wide in some cases) and power are awesome. To know wind is to fear the hurricane, since a given wind's pressure is the square of its velocity. A 200-mph wind, for example, is not simply twice but 100 times as strong as a 100-mph wind—a wind that creates terrible waves, uproots enormous trees, and blows away houses. The temperamental hurricane is destructive and deadly, spawning tornadoes and torrential rains. Galveston's hurricane of 1900 left 6,000 people dead and still stands as one of the worst disasters of the twentieth century. (*See* LIGHTNING, UMBRELLAS, WATER.)

HYPNOSIS

Hypnosis works. It worked for ancient Egyptians and Greeks, it's worked as a surgical anesthetic, and it works as a method of psychotherapy. Hypnosis induces a broad range of behavioral responses, and many of them are negative: wild hallucinations, amnesia, and sense distortions.

The hypnotized are totally smitten by their hypnotizer and respond to his suggestions absolutely, literally, uncritically. You don't have to be in a draped parlor with a Svengali-type creep: You can be hypnotized when you least expect it, by the most innocent-looking people.

Posthypnotic suggestions will have you barking like a dog, stumbling through hopscotch like the clumsiest kid, or actually blistering your skin on ice cubes you've been convinced are red-hot. Use of hypnosis could very well sidetrack real psychological and medical analysis, and, depending on the malevolence of your mesmerizer, transform you into an antisocial, even criminal, creature.

ICE

Tame ice, as in cubes, has become a safe and essential component of modern living. But wild ice, the kind that doesn't clink, is something altogether different. It takes the form of glaciers, ice sheets, and icebergs.

Glaciers advance and retreat, geologists say, about every 10,000 years—a figure the scientists have been using a suspiciously long time. The present "interglacial period" (the term itself alludes to the inevitability of new descents of ice sheets) is surely near its end, and with that will come a new ice age, an epoch of blue death. During the last one, glaciers covered Scandinavia, and extended the width of Canada south to the Great Lakes, a range of ice mountains two miles high. Nourished by snow and cold and precipitation, glaciers advance from the northern latitudes and can bulldoze continents as they make their weighty and persistent trips south. But glacial movement isn't necessarily slow. Earthquakes can shake glaciers loose, sending the masses of ice over inhabited areas of land at lightning speeds.

Glaciers are sensitive to the smallest changes in temperature; pollution's "greenhouse effect" may one day result in sudden glacial melt. Volcanic eruptions over glacial areas cause something called glacial burst which, like sudden melt, prompts floods of icy water. But glaciers don't have to move or melt to be dangerous: They are shot through with crevasses (potential graves that may be hundreds of feet deep) and are also the stomping ground of polar bears, which are strictly carnivorous and not at all afraid of us.

Icebergs of course continue to threaten ships at sea. Any structure capable of doing what the iceberg did to the *Titanic* should be avoided. (*See* WATER.)

IMPORTED POTTERY

Mexican bowls, Italian mugs, Japanese pitchers, and other imported pottery can cause constipation, anemia, emaciation, hallucinations, sterility, paralysis, even death. It's not what's in the dishes, but what's on them.

Domestic potters tend not to use lead, a major and dangerous component in the glazes used by ceramists outside the United States. The foreign pots are fine for display, flowers, or some non-acidic foods and drinks. But anything carbonated or containing vinegar, coffee or acidic juices can leach the lead from the glaze, and poison the pot.

Once ingested, lead holes up in bones, and when enough accumulates, suddenly rushes into the body's fluids. That's something to think about next time you pour coffee into your favorite souvenir mug or serve Christmas desserts on those holly dishes, which come from Japan.

INTERSTATE HIGHWAYS

Superslabs, CB radio operators call them. In fact, CB radios are an IH hazard, instilling arrogance in drivers whose necks are already a shade red. There is no way to drive safely while yakking with good buddies.

Narrow country highways keep drivers alert with their ups and downs and roadside oddities, but interstates practically induce sleep with their monotonous itineraries. All those blue and green signs direct motorists to establishments that offer no regional character, most of them being fast food joints, hazards in their own right.

INTESTINAL BYPASS SURGERY

You should be afraid of reaching a point of obesity so morbid that intestinal bypass surgery is a justified risk. It works all right, but so would severing the vocal cords to stifle gossip.

The operation is not very complicated. Eighty to ninety percent of the small intestine—that's about twenty-four feet—is simply removed, the jejunum portion sutured to the terminal section of the ileum, so that ingested substances go from the stomach almost directly into the large intestine. Fats and carbohydrates are absorbed in the small intestine, so the "malabsorption" resulting from the bypass causes an average weight loss of ten pounds per month for the six months following surgery, then six pounds per month for the next two or three years. Weight stabilizes at about 20 percent above the patient's ideal poundage.

The "last chance" surgery, which has a 5 percent mortality rate and is for all practical pruposes irreversible, has various physical and psychological side effects. There's even a disease named after it, bypass enteritis, the symptoms of which are painful and obvious: anal inflammation, severe diarrhea, flatulence, abdominal distension. Postoperative problems also include decreased levels of potassium, magnesium, B-12, calcium, protein, and an electrolyte imbalance. Protein depletion impairs the mobilization of liver fats while encouraging absorption of bile salts, total liver failure being the potential outcome. Bypass operations are also frequently followed by pneumonia.

Patients tend to have exceedingly high expectations of the evisceration, and since they usually remain somewhat plump afterwards, may get depressed. Even when the results are very good, it can be bad. Abrupt liberation from an immense body can cause a sort of ongoing giddiness, extravagance, and carelessness. A study conducted by the Universities of Wisconsin and Kentucky found that bypass operations have destroyed marriages. Most of it has to do with a suddenly-slim person's rediscovery of their romantic self, so long trapped in folds of skin. Though that would seem to be a boon to relationships, it apparently throws them out of kilter.

J

JOGGING

In 490 B.C., Pheidippides ran 20 miles from Marathon to Athens, announced the Greek victory over Persia, then promptly fell over dead. Few joggers have met that fate, but other dangers are common to the track, from shin splints and heel spurs to sagging breasts and spleen damage. Jogging is now the punishment for 30 million American feet which are reverberating brutal shocks throughout runners' bodies.

It's no wonder that jogging hurts—the average runner's bony feet pound the running surface at the rate of 15,000 times per hour, each footfall a shock that loosens internal organs, tears ligaments, and splinters bones.

The prognosis for runners includes:

—heat exhaustion;
—sacroiliac injuries;
—slipped discs;
—fallen arches;
—jiggled and sloshed spleen, kidneys, and uterus;
—tendon inflammation;
—blisters and bruises.

Running exceptionally long distances does such violence to veins in the legs that phlebitis and blood clots can occur after a masochistic marathon.

City runners often have to deal with the added impact of concrete surfaces, wiseacre motorists, and territorial dogs.

JULY AND AUGUST

In addition to snakebites, fatal insect stings, and sunburns, July and August also usher in the year's most burglaries, assaults, rapes, and murders.

K

KARAKORAM HIGHWAY

The Karakoram Highway, which roughly follows Marco Polo's "silk route" across southern Asia, cuts into the Himalayas and at some points is 18,000 feet above sea level. That's over 3 precarious miles high. Nearly 3,000 people died during construction of the high highway, and you can bet that lots will die traveling it. There's actually a landslide crew assigned to the 540-mile road, and its work is especially vital during the monsoon.

L

LACTATING MOTHERS

Tending their litters, mothers have in common a fierce instinct to protect their sucklings, and will make unprovoked attacks to do so. There's an old story of a sow gobbling up a child who had innocently approached the hog to get a better look at her pink piglets.

LARGE CARS

All the talk about small cars being deathmobiles is wrong; large cars are the ones unsafe at any speed. Sure, small cars are lightweight and short-nosed, features that facilitate crush, but they are also nimble, human-scaled, and keep drivers in touch with their surroundings.

Large cars are capable of incredible speed, dangerous in itself, and are comfortable and insulated to the point of being soporific. Their drivers cannot help but feel invulnerable behind those imposing dashboards, and, surrounded by all the comforts of home, drowsy. The heralded "quiet ride" is a death trip—drivers shouldn't be made oblivious to the sounds and sights of the road.

LEGIONNAIRES' DISEASE

Like something out of a science fiction scenario, this pneumonia-like plague, one of the great modern medical mysteries, decimates confined populations. Hundreds of cases of Legionnaires' Disease have been reported since its first outbreak in Philadelphia in 1976 that killed 29

American Legion conventioneers. The disease usually kills 15 percent of its victims, many of whom don't even have time to get to their doctors, so rapidly do body temperatures rise and air passages collapse.

Scientists have isolated the bacterium, a new one for the books that seems to be air-borne, non-contagious, and fond of clustering in specific environments (hotels, neighborhoods). No one knows exactly where and how the germ exists, or whence it came.

LICORICE

Excessive consumption of natural licorice—it comes from a flowering plant of Europe and Asia—can raise blood pressure. Licorice is not only the main ingredient of the popular candy, but is also used as a flavoring in various drugs—which may therefore counteract high blood pressure medication.

LIGHTNING

Lightning is fascinating and dazzling but mostly frightening: It's killed more people than tornadoes or hurricanes. There's really very little to prevent your becoming the unfortunate conductor of a bolt of lightning shot down from one of about 1,800 thunderstorms raging over the earth this very minute.

The giant cumulonimbus cloud, or thunderhead, mother of tornadoes, also gives birth to lightning. In *The Lightning Book,* Peter E. Viemeister describes a thunderhead as an "ordinary cumulus cloud gone wild . . . a huge storm factory, a monstrous atmospheric machine with the energy of an atom bomb." During a storm, clouds become highly charged with either negative or positive electricity, and 90 percent of all lightning discharges harmlessly high above. But we must contend with the other 10 percent.

Every object jutting from the earth's surface—from a building to your hair—becomes highly ionized, and if the thunderhead's electrical stream makes contact with an opposite earthbound charge, a path is opened and wham! Lightning strikes in a split second. (A new theory proposes that lightning is caused by rays from outer space, and not by simple interactions between storm clouds and the ground. But whether lightning's origins are cosmic or not doesn't lessen its threat.)

A direct strike could paralyze your nervous system, causing instantaneous death. Indirect strikes are more common, and usually result in severe burns. And despite what Smokey the Bear says, lightning is responsible for most forest and grass fires.

Survivors of lightning strikes don't have fond memories of their confrontation with the avalanche of electrons. One said it felt like he was slugged over the head by a giant hammer. Another victim was temporarily blinded, her ring melted on her finger, and her ears rang for days.

The cautious will avoid Daytona Beach, Florida, since lightning is more likely to strike there than anywhere else. (*See* UMBRELLAS.)

LOCKJAW

Tetanus, like botulism, is the malevolent work of an anaerobic *Clostridium* bacterium. The disease, commonly known as lockjaw, is acute, highly infectious, and far too accessible: The slightest abrasion leaves a body open for attack by tetanospasmin, one of the deadliest neurotoxins known. Lockjaw is characterized by rigidity and spasms of the voluntary muscles, and when those of the jaws are involved, as they frequently are, the victim cannot perform two vital functions: eating and crying out for help.

M

MANHOOD

Being male should worry a fellow. There are eight good reasons.

1. Three out of four murder victims are men.
2. Two-thirds of those admitted to hospital emergency rooms are men.
3. Men commit suicide more often than women.
4. For a long time to come, male will be the sex, voluntarily or not, that goes to war.
5. Snakes and lightning rarely strike women.
6. Most alcoholics are men.
7. Hemochromotosis, a rare and debilitating toxicity to iron, most often afflicts men.
8. Puberty rites are painful.

MARCH

Beware the ides of March, yes, but also the fortnights preceding and following it.

March is a bad month, ravaged by tornadoes, blizzards, and floods.

Mumps, measles, and meningococcal infections are reported most often in March, and hepatitis frequently adds to the month's bad medical news.

March also seems to be a time of negative contemplation: Most suicides occur in the two months that follow it, April and May.

MEAT

Of all the reasons to be afraid of eating, meat is one of the most convincing. The average American eats more beef and veal than sugar (that's over 100 pounds annually), and the chemically and naturally contaminatèd animal flesh requires an exhausting effort to digest.

Meat is the most common source of food poisoning. Even so-called organically-raised livestock harbors a number of diseases, including trichinosis, brucellosis, and salmonosis. Raw meat is especially dangerous, so no matter how smart it seems, never order steak Tartare.

Meat procured through the usual channels—from the butcher or supermarket—carries the added danger of chemical additives and preservatives. Upton Sinclair described it as "embalmed beef." Livestock are fed and shot full of antibiotics, enzymes, and about a dozen different hormones—"growth promoters," the industry calls them. The hormones used are of female endocrine and their presence in meat has been found to be carcinogenic and capable of causing sterility in men.

The journey from steer to steak involves ranchers, slaughterhouse personnel, truckers, processors, and government inspectors who have undeservedly won public confidence. Each handling threatens the health of the carnivorous consumer, particularly the stop made for nitrite, which is used to cure the meat and give it the red color that enhances not flavor but sales. Ham, pastrami, bologna, corned beef, sausages, and bacon are all cured with nitrite, a chemical that combines in the stomach with amines (which are in practically everything else ingested) to form nitrosamines. Nitrosamines cause cancer. The industry is reluctant to do away with nitrite (safer substances would work as well), convinced as the public is that redder meat is better meat.

Something else about meat: Big bites of it are the usual cause of "cafe coronary," the unfortunate incidence of food lodging in a diner's throat, blocking air passage. Though its simple first aid maneuver has been widely demonstrated, cafe coronary kills about 4,000 people each year. Non-fatal cases usually result in irreversible brain damage, caused by a mere four minutes without oxygen.

METEORITES

While meteorites are not one of life's great threats, the cautious should still occasionally glance skyward. Created when asteroids collide, meteors are chunks of stone and iron that tumble through space and time. If they should enter earth's atmosphere, and countless thousands do every year, and fall to earth, which much fewer do, they are known as meteorites.

This dangerous debris from space has been recorded since the dawn of civilization. Ancients believed that meteorites, whose fall to earth is often a spectacular audio-visual experience, were sent by the gods. But people didn't always believe they could exist. Between the mid-eighteenth and mid-nineteenth centuries, few could see room in the Newtonian universe for space rocks. One theory held that meteorites were made of volcanic dust, coagulated in mid-air by lightning. Scientific theories, however, began to change about the time meteor showers were being recorded, such as the immense fall over L'Aigle, France in 1807. The thundering fireballs traveling at supersonic speeds were hard to ignore, and meteorites were soon accepted as natural phenomena.

How afraid should you be of bombardment? Meteorites can be as big as boulders, so they are certainly capable of damaging people, animals, structures, and landscape. The famous Meteor Crater in Arizona, dating from prehistoric times, is 600 feet deep and 4,000 feet across. The largest known meteorite to fall in modern times landed in South Africa in 1920, and weighs 60 tons. In 1948, a shower of one-ton stones pelted much of Norton County, Kansas. A lady in Alabama was badly bruised when a meteorite tore through the roof of her house in 1954 and hit her thigh. Calves, goats, and dogs have been crushed by large meteorites. A 47-square-mile area in Argentina was cratered by meteorites that destroyed small shacks, and the stones have also shattered windows and smashed into automobiles. Meteor showers have also leveled small stands of trees.

Considering the fact that one in 66 meteorites will strike a densely populated area, it is surprising that there are so few accidents, and no reported fatalities in modern times. The chance of a U.S. citizen being struck is one in 9,300. Indications are, however, that meteor showers are increasing.

Since there's nothing to stop a meteor from slamming into a spacecraft, you should also be afraid of space travel. And never touch a meteorite: It might be contaminated. Unfriendly organisms from the far reaches of the galaxies can hitch a ride to our planet on a meteor, and there is some evidence of this occurring: Amino acids with no known biological business on earth have been found in meteorites, as have traces of radioactive material.

All of the dangers of real meteorites are applicable to man-made meteorites such as the remains of Skylab, which only by luck did not fall on Times Square.

MEXICAN JAILS

Conditions vary, but Mexican jails, according to their inmates, are unsanitary, buzzing with flies, jumping with fleas, and run by sadistic bullies. The guards, like Mexico's laws, are especially hard on young Americans accused of—or framed with—drug trafficking, and take a savage interest in punishing the prisoners during their interminable incarcerations.

Refugees recount among their Mexican jail experience Russian roulette, hard labor, and rape. Some tell of having their heads crammed down toilets, and earrings torn from their pierced earlobes. One young prisoner said he was stripped, shackled to a shower head, and tortured with an electric cattle prod, an apparently popular routine among the thuggish officials. The treatment is about the same for first as repeat offenders, and no consideration is made for possession of a single joint as opposed to a pound.

The food in the prisons is so bad and so ridden with disease-carrying bacteria that if prisoners don't send out for meals (at their own expense), they'll suffer food poisoning.

MICROWAVES

That microwaves are harmful to us is beyond question, and it's no secret that those most economically dependent on the electromagnetic radiation—the armed forces and the home appliance industry—are lying about the radiation threat.

Microwave radiation ("electronic smog," to environmentalists) pulsates from the usual intimidating sources such as the military's massive radar systems and medicine's diathermy machines, but also from seemingly innocuous ones, such as CB radios, burglar alarms, automatic doors, and microwave ovens. Microwaves are seldom perfectly contained in whatever gadget—ovens are particularly susceptible to leakage. (*Consumer Reports* doesn't recommend a single one for this reason.) The effects of microwave radiation—which is actually much stronger than the sun's natural emissions—are beginning to show.

Just as they blast a roast by super-exciting its molecules, microwaves are capable of roasting people. Even low-level radiation has caused headaches, dizziness, and blood strangeness. Microwaves can interfere with pacemakers. Radar technicians have developed cataracts on the back of the eyeball, where only the insidious microwaves can reach. Most frightening of all is recent evidence of radiation-damaged chromosomes, which we see as birth defects among children of the army's radiation personnel. The Veterans Administration is now making disability payments to microwave victims, which rather antagonizes the army's insistent denials of radiation risk.

MOTORCYCLES

Motorcycles have long been the preferred means of transportation of people you shouldn't trust. Members of Hell's Angels, the Bandidos, and other brotherhoods that wage gang war rely heavily on the fierce imagery of straddling big, powerful bikes. Those who opt for the two-wheelers are people inordinately thrilled by noise, speed, and acute turns, which, in force, are highway hell. Since over half the states have repealed their helmet laws, motorcycle fatalities have increased nationally as much as 35 percent. The really shocking thing is that it's no longer unheard-of, in a given reporting period, for more people to be killed on bikes than in cars. (*See* BALLPOINT PENS.)

MOUNTAINEERING

Mountaineering involves mountains, which are frightening because they are there: tall; craggy; low on oxygen; cold; home to wildcats, wolves, and vultures; the deliverers of avalanches, landslides, and icefalls; and, in many cases, covered with slippery lemming droppings.

Mountaineering, which dates from the early nineteenth century, is dangerous for the above reasons, and because it requires group effort, something not cheerily had these days. Mountaineers stick together, so, in avalanches and landslides, they die together. A slide in Switzerland last century buried 500 people, and in 1962 an avalanche on Mount Huascaran in Peru dumped 13,000,000 cubic yards of snow and ice on Ranrahirca and six other surrounding villages.

Great geologic catastrophes make mountains, orogenesis entailing much heaving of and sputtering forth from the earth's crust. These violent building processes are signals to leave mountains alone; they are no place for people.

MUSHROOMS

Mushrooms can provide a good meal, visions, or death, so foraging for the fungi is one of the riskier ways to spend an afternoon.

Some of the most gorgeous mushrooms—"the food of the gods" to the Romans—are the most deadly, such as the tall and graceful *Amanita phalloides,* alias Destroying Angel alias Death Cap. About 90 percent of all deaths attributed to mushroom poisoning point back to this most murderous fungus, which is abundant worldwide.

The Destroying Angel contains five separate toxins, heat-stable proteins which, upon entering your bloodstream, do terrible and irreversible work on your kidneys, liver, and central nervous system. The symptoms develop slowly. Six to fifteen hours after you've savored one, you experience stomach pain, nausea, vomiting, incredible thirst, inability to urinate, exhaustion, jaundice, and convulsions. Within a week, you enter a coma and die.

Only an expert mycologist can tell the gourmet from the deadly; the rule or test doesn't exist that can absolutely detect the killers. Only non-toxic mushrooms, for instance, are said to have caps whose skin will peel off, but Destroying Angel's comes off in a neat layer. To add to the confusion, toxicity levels in the bad ones can change with ecologies. Some poisonous mushrooms will lose their toxin when cooked, salted, or dried; others won't.

Two species of non-toxic mushrooms are now found to contain natural carcinogenic compounds. The discovery was made by the University of Nebraska's Eppley Institute, and the American Mushroom Institute isn't happy about the publication of the findings. The mushrooms in question are the False Morel, often sold in gourmet shops, and the Common Mushroom, 350 million pounds of which are sold each year in the U.S. alone, mostly through supermarkets. Both species contain hydrazines, which have caused lung and blood-vessel cancer in test animals.

It's not known yet whether the hydrazines can survive a sauté.

N

NEGATIVE HEELS

The shoes that set people back on their heels are rooted in the unalarming fact that when one stands in wet sand, the heel sinks lower than the ball of the foot. Various manufacturers of the titled footwear did not give much thought to an equally obvious fact, that few people spend much time standing in wet sand.

Shoes should not indulge bad posture, but do all they can to support tired feet (each of which contains twenty-six bones). Negative heels work against the efficiency of the arch, and put pressure on the muscles of the back and legs. The overall effect of negative heels is a reduction in the distance one is able to gracefully and painlessly walk.

NERVE GAS

Nerve gas is more than a bad memory from World War II—20,000 tons of it are in frighteningly fragile storage all across America, with Utah, Colorado, and Alabama holding particularly large arsenals.

Nerve gas is an organic compound that zaps the enzymes vital to the transmission of signals throughout the nervous system. It's odorless, so it is usually inhaled in ignorance. Death does not come peacefully: Victims vomit and convulse wildly.

We could breathe easier if the gas was sitting tight in its tanks and cannisters. But it has leaked since the 1940s and may again. The contents of a small container could kill people a mile away. Warehouses of nerve gas are structurally flawed and fraught with security problems, making them vulnerable to theft by terrorists. When the stockpiles of gas are transported, they are done so by rail, a discomforting situation with train derailments a fearsome fact of life.

THE NEUTRON BOMB

The neutron bomb is touted as a sort of gentleman's weapon, in that it lessens the chance of killing unintended victims and preserves architecture. These are arguments that could also be put forth for chemical warfare, which proved to be so inhumane during World War II that it was internationally outlawed. Neutron proponents also contend that the "enhanced radiation warhead" is economical, its range of destruction being specific, and that its aftermath won't too strongly affect the environment. These points are debatable to begin with, and the whole pitch has the perverse effect of making war sound like a bankable investment.

The basic idea of a neutron bomb has been kicked around since the 1940s, and it was actually formulated in 1958, the product of a relatively simple fission-fusion reaction. Upon detonation, fission triggers fusion, which releases neutrons. The superfast neutrons, the particles that "enhance" the radiation, would collide with protons in animal cells, breaking down chromosomes, deforming cell nuclei, thickening cell fluids, and, the real clincher, impairing mitosis, the process of cell division that could possibly reverse the damage. The subsequent human response would be weird: Death is certain, but it'd take a while and would surely come painfully. If victims could walk, they'd essentially be walking dead, zombies.

Even beyond its target area, the neutron bomb would create thermal radiation sufficient to cause second-degree burns, and its residual fallout may produce leukemia, cataracts, and genetic damage—but would let stand the buildings, the telephone poles, and the works of art.

NEVADA

Where should one go in the United States to snap out of a funk? Not to Nevada, where the suicide rate is the nation's highest. The gamblers' state has been number one for years, followed by Arizona, Alaska and California.

The West, though, isn't despair's exclusive domain; Vermont, Florida and Michigan also have higher-than-average suicide rates.

NOVAS

Novas are stars that suddenly multiply their surface luminosities by factors of thousands, in impetuous bursts of energy, light, and ultra-violet radiation that have profound effects on the heavens. Born of quiet little stars, novas are sort of like unassuming people who suddenly turn criminally insane. (Supernovas are a hundred times more demonstrative than the brightest novas since their explosion usually involves the entire mass of the star.) About 50 novas occur each year in our galaxy. A star itself, our sun could become a nova, an event that would destroy earth in a few hours.

NUKES

Nuclear power, born of fission, is fueled by enriched uranium's yield of plutonium, one of the world's deadliest substances, and the critical component of nuclear bombs. Nuclear power plants, which house this atom-splitting activity and its dreaded by-products, are notoriously vulnerable to piracy. A large reactor produces an annual radioactive surplus sufficient to manufacture a thousand Hiroshima bombs, and hundreds of pounds of these poisons have been stolen. Nuclear weaponry has more benevolent origins, too: America's naive "Atoms for Peace" program, whereby uranium-to-plutonium technology and materials were made widely available, accounts for India and other countries having developed the bomb.

Radioactive wastes, which are particularly copious from fast-breeder reactors, accumulate at every stage of the so-called nuclear fuel cycle, and remain toxic for 500,000 years. (The nuclear fuel cycle is not a cycle at all, since its elements never return to a benign state.) How to get rid of this hot nuclear garbage, whose leakage would essentially ionize the food chain, has puzzled scientists, thwarted utility companies, and enraged everyone concerned about their health. Proposed and abandoned: storage in underground tanks, ocean dumps, burial under Antarctic ice sheets, shooting the wastes into the sun. Fact is, there is no way to store or dispose of nuclear materials that is not economically, technologically, politically, and especially ecologically problematic. So, each year, 2,000 tons of radioactive trash are added to the U.S. nuclear heaps, at the mercy of storms, corrosion, mad bombers, and seismic disturbances (some caused by underground nuclear tests).

Nukes have fallen far short of their promise of abundant energy cheaply had. Nineteen countries generate marginal amounts of electricity from nuclear sources, including the United States, whose 63 plants meet no more than 3 percent of the country's energy needs.

But there is no question of nukes' ability to deliver environmental wallops. Even their relatively simple cooling systems, which return water to its source as much as 40 degrees hotter than normal, are responsible for destroying fish, shellfish, and plant life. It looks like nuclear pollution may be the worst of all. Health, Education and Welfare studies indicate a cancerous relationship between people and their proximity to nuclear power plants: Cancer-related deaths are rising faster in states with busy nuclear facilities—Connecticut, Tennessee, Pennsylvania and South Carolina, for example—than in areas with the highest levels of more "traditional" pollution.

NYLON UNDERWEAR

An ammonia-based synthesis of carbon, hydrogen, nitrogen, and oxygen, nylon is a thermoinsulating material, which means that nylon underwear holds heat and moisture against the body, compounding and prolonging, among a host of others, vaginal infections.

O

OIL SPILLS

Oil on the sea, as in the notorious spill at Union Oil's Platform A off Santa Barbara on January 28, 1969, does immediate damage to marine and coastal life: doomed birds made heavy and flightless; plant life smothered; fish and shellfish suffocated. The toxic detergents used to break up the grease have a long-range effect on the ecosystem by upsetting the ocean's chemistry and thwarting predator-prey relationships and reproduction. Human ingestion of the contaminated victims of oil spills is inevitable, so there is justified alarm over the continual increase in oil being pumped from the ocean floor and transported across seas.

OLEANDERS

Landscape architects have made a big mistake in their rampant use of the oleander, for the tall, flowering bush carries a toxin that goes straight for the heart. But there they are, in parks, along freeways, and around public buildings, particularly in southern California and along the Gulf Coast. Large animals have died from grazing on oleanders, and in 1961, 34 Florida flamingos flopped over dead after nibbling on a single plant.

You don't have to eat leaves to get hit. Honey made from oleander nectar is highly poisonous, a burning bush produces deadly smoke, and meat skewered on its branches absorbs a full load of toxin. Hot dogs pierced on oleander sticks will guarantee that no one returns from the weenie roast.

ORGAN BUILDERS

Don't bother mail-ordering these expensive and worthless gadgets, less euphemistically known as breast and penis enlargers. Equal damage to the body part in question can be achieved with an ordinary vacuum cleaner. The people who make these things are actually paying their rent, having exploited popular delusions about physical endowment. Breast enlargers, which look rather like funnels for gasoline tanks, brutalize ligaments; penis enlargers, resembling oversized test tubes, can rupture blood vessels. Both tend to desensitize whatever protuberance they're attached to.

ORTHOPEDICS

It is hard to understand devotees of orthopedics, people who like having their backs realigned like the front ends of automobiles. Muscles are quite enough to support the skeletal system, and good posture will keep backs as straight as they need to be. Patients of back doctors, though, are all but addicted to having their delicate vertebrae popped and jabbed, and it's all too close to the spinal cord for comfort.

P

PCP/ANGEL DUST

Veterinarians rarely put PCP (phencyclidine) to its single legal use as an animal tranquilizer—which they did in the tragic case of Bubbles the hippopotamus—but 7,000,000 fearless American youth, mostly white kids from cities and suburbs, are snorting and smoking the stuff like crazy. Some have died. Its makers are pleased: Angel Dust is the fastest-growing drug of abuse in the adolescent market. The average Angel Duster is 15 years old.

Easily manufactured in home laboratories, Angel Dust is far from heaven, and the artificial substance seems to be a potion for sadomasochism. One PCP user yanked out his teeth with pliers. One stabbed a baby boy and his pregnant mother. After smoking PCP, one young man clawed out his eyes to escape from horrifying hallucinations. Other users have shot strangers, drowned in inches of water, and one drank poison to kill the rats he believed were in his stomach.

Though many admit the drug's high is terrifying, they inexplicably return for more. Researchers say it acts on the sensory cortex, thalamus, and midbrain, scrambling the body's messages to the brain and depressing the central nervous system. Speech and hearing loss often result, as well as delirium and muscle rigidity. Heart and respiratory failure may bring death. Trace amounts may lodge in the brain, which is particularly dangerous since the drug's toxicity is chiefly behavioral, producing something amazingly like paranoid schizophrenia.

"Angel Dust" is certainly one of the drug world's more alluring euphemisms. People might be less willing to try it if they knew its other, more appropriate, names: embalming fluid, goon, killer weed, rocket fuel, horse tranquilizer.

PASTEURIZED AND HOMOGENIZED MILK

Though they are often wrong in their insistence that anything packaged in natural shades of brown is good for you, the health food people are right about milk.

The high heat required of the pasteurization process renders milk worthless and harmful. Pasteurization destroys phosphatase, an important enzyme; lysine, listidine, and other amino acids that would assist digestion of the milk; vitamin A; and 38 percent of the vitamin B-complex. Pasteurized milk's scant amount of vitamin C and reduced levels of soluble calcium have been linked to scurvy and maldevelopment of bones and teeth in infants.

Homogenization breaks up and disperses milk's fat globules, making them much too absorbable by the bloodstream. The body's defense against the invasion of milk fats results in bad scarring of the arteries, called atherosclerosis, which can lead to stroke and heart attack.

PAVULON

Pavulon is a prescription drug specifically used to stop the breathing of patients as they're placed on artificial respirators. Like other drugs, it has turned up outside of hospitals. One doctor has described non-medical use of Pavulon as a live burial, since a person injecting it remains alert but unbreathing, a sort of suicide by suffocation.

PAY TOILETS

People have missed planes because of jammed doors on pay toilets. Worse than that, for lack of a dime some have tumbled onto tile floors and suffered concussions trying to climb in and out of the vending stalls.

PENNSYLVANIA

Pennsylvania was bailed out with more federal disaster assistance between 1972 and 1977 than any other state, so something there is clearly out of whack. That government assistance—a whopping $304,530,000—went for the incredible amount of destruction wrought by a series of severe storms, including the nation's worst floods. Then came 1979's near-meltdown at the Three Mile Island nuclear power plant.

Only the foolhardy would live in Pennsylvania, a state prone to disaster and whose ability to recover and rescue is less than inspiring.

PET TURTLES

Those little green turtles sold in some pet shops are effective transmitters of salmonella, the food-poisoning germ. (*See* WOODEN CUTTING BOARDS.)

THE PILL

It is incredible that a drug used by so many millions for so long carries this warning on its labels: "Oral contraceptives are powerful and effective drugs which can cause side effects in some users and should not be used at all by some women. The most serious known side effect is abnormal clotting which can be fatal."

The pill has been linked to many conditions, which are compounded if a woman smokes cigarettes, is overweight, drinks even moderate amounts of alcohol, or takes other prescription drugs. In 1976, Planned Parenthood reported that women 40 years and older risk pill-related death twenty times more than younger women.

Even the most prudent user of the pill stands to be toppled by blood clots, heart attacks, and strokes. The pill also affects weight (since estrogen acts on fat molecules) and raises serum cholesterol and blood pressure. Liver and particularly breast cancer are frequently reported among those who take the pill.

Granted, the pill is 99 percent effective in controlling birth, but its side effects—and the uterine infections associated with IUDs—strongly suggest that it is time to apply birth control experimentation, for which women have been virtual guinea pigs since 1961, to men. (*See* STEROIDS.)

PINK FLUORESCENT LIGHTS

Not that it's being used much anymore, but indirect lighting of various colors was what the 1950s contributed to offbeat interior decorating. Now we've learned that fluorescent lighting causes hyperkinetic behavior, insomnia, and headaches—consequences, scientists hypothesize, of ultra-violet radiation and mercury vapors emitted from the tubes of light. These risks are greater at the strong orange-pink end of the spectrum.

PLATFORM SHOES

Six or so inches is a considerable distance for a heel to fall, and platform shoes have caused aching ankles, fractured feet, and splintered shins.

POLYCHLORINATED BIPHENYLS

Polychlorinated biphenyls: Two unattractive words that should be in your vocabulary since they are very likely in your body. PCBs, formidable members of the dreaded chlorinated hydrocarbon family, are synthetic organic chemicals used as cooling agents in electrical equipment. Other industries also find them irreplaceable: PCBs are used to process paints, oils, adhesives, and various packaging materials. PCBs are manufactured in Great Britain, France, Germany, the USSR, Japan, Spain, Italy, Czechoslovakia, and by the Monsanto Chemical Company in the United States. The result of all this is that PCBs are among the most widespread and abundant contaminants on earth.

They are released into the environment via effluence, vaporation, or combustion. From earth, wind, and fire, then, PCBs move up the food chain, ultimately lodging in human tissues and fat; they now reside in food supplies, wildlife, and especially in marine and fresh-water fish. PCBs are in virtually everything we eat and drink.

PCBs have rendered fish sterile. The chemicals have migrated from packaging materials into feed, ultimately killing millions of chickens. Their effect on primates seems to be mental disorders. A 1968 epidemic of chloracne, a skin disease, broke out in Japan, and was subsequently linked to the victims' consumption of rice oil tainted with PCBs.

POLYESTER

Polyester fibers are products of petroleum and natural gas—nonrenewable energy supplies whose continued procurement poisons the food chain and the atmosphere. Granted, synthetics require little maintenance, but they don't "breathe" the way natural fabrics do. Which means that when worn in very hot weather, polyester could cause heat strokes, or at least such discomfort that one might lose control of oneself, precipitating any number of predicaments.

POPPERS

When poppers first came on the market in the mid-1970s, "Gaynip" was proposed by two shrewd New Yorkers as the ultimate brand name. One of the cheapest and shortest thrills ever, poppers (amyl nitrite if you have a doctor friend who'll write you a prescription, isobutyl nitrite if not) initially became the gay rage and, like Village People, soon caught on in the straight market as well.

Makers of Bolt, Rush, and Locker Room, 3 brands of the legal isobutyl nitrite, estimate that 5 million Americans regularly sniff the flammable liquid that *Time* magazine has called the "poor man's cocaine."

By dilating blood vessels and lowering blood pressure, poppers produce a few euphoric seconds and a sort of pounding in the brain that can pass for excitement. They seem to encourage people to do things they'd be better off not doing, like having sex with dolts who probably carry gonorrhea or lurking around ear-blasting discos.

Excessive use of poppers can result in at least the headache of a lifetime, and they're so rough on nasal membranes you'll swear your nose will fall off. Some experiments have linked them to heart attacks, liver disease, and lung damage.

POTTER

The largest hailstones on record pelted the western Nebraska town of Potter in 1928. The chunks of precipitated ice were about 5.5 inches in diameter, and weighed nearly two pounds. Hail like that could crack skulls.

PRE-SURGICAL SHAVING

As if surgery itself isn't enough to send you into fits of anxiety, researchers have found that the time-honored practice of shaving a surgical site prior to an operation leaves the patient open to bacterial infections. Since its elimination of routine shaving, the Foothills Hospital in Calgary has achieved the lowest surgical infection rate of any other hospital in the world.

A study at the Canadian hospital showed that patients who were shaved suffered a post-surgical infection rate of 2.7 percent; those who weren't shaved, 0.9 percent. Showering before an operation with an antibacterial soap is all that's necessary.

PUBLIC SERVICE ADVERTISING

It is perhaps the height of cynicism to distrust Smokey the Bear, but his creators are not living up to their promise to contribute advertising for the public good. Public service advertisements are created free of charge by advertising agencies, and are published and broadcast gratuitously by the media; you've seen them in the back pages of magazines and on non-prime-time television. It's a billion-dollar business with potential for real public service, so it's a shame that the public service campaigns are used by advertisers to clear their collective guilty conscience and to protect the industrial giants whose products and services are detrimental to the so-called public good.

How can you find fault with an enterprise that measures its success not in profits but in donations, public safety, college enrollments, volunteer recruits, and energy and lives saved? Easy. Public service advertising is self-serving in its diversion of attention from the rascals really responsible for what it deems our most urgent social and economic ills. For example, powerless consumers are scolded in condescending ads that announce that careless campers, not the timber industry, are responsible for vanishing forests, and that unbuckled seat belts, rather than shoddily-built cars, are to blame for rising traffic fatalities. They slap the hands of littering citizens, but say nothing to polluting industries. And how seriously can we take anti-smoking messages from companies that hold lucrative contracts with tobacco conglomerates?

The people who produce public service ads are the same whose livelihood depends on good sales of paper and lumber, automobiles, cigarettes, and scores of other products that have created the mess that "ads in the public interest" propose to clean up.

Don't let public service advertising give you a guilt complex. It's propaganda for big business' continued pollution, depletion of natural resources, and marketing of unsafe products—things advertisers spend most of their time selling, then pretend to un-sell in bleeding-heart public service messages.

PUMPING IRON

Exercise should serve the cardiovascular system, but all pumping iron does is make rocky muscles and bulging veins. Bulging veins are veins reaching out for help. Weightlifting also works against limberness, so bodybuilders have a hard time reaching behind to swat poisonous insects and disarm muggers.

R

RADIOPHARMACEUTICALS

There are some remedies worse than the disease.

—*Publilius Syrus*

Any medicine controlled by the Nuclear Regulatory Commission shouldn't even be used on armadillos, but over 10,000,000 people in the United States have been treated with radiopharmaceuticals since their development in the late 1950s.

Radiopharmaceuticals are the tools of what's known as nuclear medicine—more of those "atoms for peace" hard at work. The ingredients involved are a number of isotopes made radioactive by neutron bombardment; iodine, calcium, strontium, cobalt, and even gold are used. The isotopes are used primarily as tracers in diagnosis, but physicians and physicists have also put them to therapeutic use, the most common being for thyroid problems. When patients drink the "atomic cocktails," the wildly unstable isotopes destroy what are hoped to be only the diseased cells.

Because they are taken orally, radiopharmaceuticals seem safer than surgery, but they're not. Leukemia is one of their risks, and you don't even want to think about the horrors of an overdose.

RATS

It is a fact that rats do attack. A man once found a rat in his infant son's crib, but instead of being frightened away, the rat went for the man's throat, then leapt on his wife. The rodents are getting meaner and braver all the time.

Rats have endured various extermination programs, and seem to have few requirements of habitat: They'll adapt to anything, and have overrun farms, cities and ships at sea. Explosively reproductive, their U.S. population is somewhere around 100,000,000.

Economic damage from the rodents is staggering. They destroy industrial equipment, take over warehouses, spoil crops, and their need to gnaw (they must, to contain their ever-growing teeth) knows no bounds. Rats even eat electrical wiring, which has caused terrible fires. Two million pounds of sugar were once spoiled by rat urine, no great nutritional loss, but offensive nonetheless.

These consequences, however, are merciful when compared to the health hazards of rats and their parasites. Rat fleas are responsible for bubonic plague, the "Black Death" that wiped out 75 million people in the fourteenth century, and which still occurs today (in fact, there's been an upsurge of the plague in the U.S. since 1974). Rats also inflict typhus, infectious jaundice, rat-bite fever, and rabies.

RED FOOD

It had to happen that red dye no. 2, banned in 1976, would be replaced by food processors with another red that, like its infamous predecessor, is a suspected poison. Red no. 40, the coloring in soda pop, candy, gelatins, barbecue sauce, pastries, pet food, sausage, and pancake mix, has been shown in all laboratory tests to be carcinogenic.

RED TIDES

No one has any business venturing near the sea anyway, but if you're willing to risk hurricanes and sharks, at least watch for a change in the water to a brownish-red color, commonly known as red tide. Cinnamon seas indicate a dinoflagellate population explosion, cause unknown, and in such huge concentrations (about 50,000,000 protozoans per liter), they release a toxic substance that is lethal to marine life, and irritating to the human respiratory system.

Red tides occur worldwide in warm ocean waters. In 1947, thousands of fish died in global red tides, and ruddy waters off the coast of England killed as many birds in 1968. (*See* WATER.)

REFUSE BINS

Those huge garbage cans on wheels are particularly dangerous to curious climbing children, who get trapped inside. One model, with an extended outer lip, giving it a boat shape, is very unstable and can easily tip over. There are also cases of runaway refuse—you wouldn't want to meet a bin as it's racing downhill.

REGIONAL MAGAZINES

The rise of regional magazines is one of the great successes of modern journalism. *Vermont Life, Southern Living, New Mexico Magazine, The Washingtonian, Nevada,* and scores of others share an editorial pitch, and it is one that tends to fragment the country. Boosters of their regions, these slick magazines promulgate chauvinism, nurture prejudices, and otherwise fan the fires of geographic feuds and civic jealousies. Reinforced by special-interest publications catering to certain avocations and professions, regional magazines are the new secessionist pamphlets, and their bluster could ultimately lead to civil war.

RETIREMENT

When folks retire, they are hit by an avalanche of wily mail-order propositions: insurance deals, travel packages, funeral and burial arrangements, shoddy condominium developments. The wise retiree will promptly incinerate this junk, so as not to compound the economic woes of retirement, precipitated in the first place by paltry government assistance programs, fixed incomes, anachronistic pensions, and new social security regulations, all bound in so much red tape that only retired accountants can figure them out. Government monies aren't the only ones denied the retired; even men and women with excellent credit histories find, upon retirement, that they cannot secure bank loans for vacations or home improvements.

Retirement takes many forms, but the one most vaunted—a move to a warm region—is in fact the most dangerous. The feather-bedded, or rather chaise longued, "sunshine retirements" of Arizona and Florida offer no stimuli, no challenges. Its customers (for that is what the retirees are) migrate down with their paperbacks and flop in the sun. Sensations soon fade, life ceases to challenge, and the body atrophies. This could have something to do with Florida and Arizona's consistent ranking among the top suicide states.

Better to retire to a cold northern climate, where each day would require a new idea, a new strategy for basic survival.

RICH PEOPLE

In revolutionary times, the rich are always the people who are most afraid.
　　　　　　　　　　　　　　　　　　　—Gerald White Johnson

They've been called different, but rich people are also dangerous. Psychiatrists say that rich kids are chronically depressed and bored and attempt to buy happiness—which is always a raw deal—and embark on crazy pursuits of pleasure and excitement—which get them into all sorts of legal and medical trouble. Moneyed people, able to afford the fastest cars and the finest Scotch, can hurt themselves as badly as anyone in their way.

Everyone, though, wants to be rich and will endanger you to become so. Therefore, exercise caution in the company of poor folks as well.

RINGS

Since fingers are the first to go in an accident, rings are virtual lures to danger. A little girl once fell from a chain-link fence, caught her finger on the top wire and stripped her middle finger to the bone. Then there was the time a ladder collapsed under a man who was hanging a picture: He fell to the floor minus one finger, which his ring hung on the wall.

At least 200 Americans lose fingers in ring accidents every year, and for each of these there are about ten other less serious ring accidents. "I wish we could convey to the public that they should get their rings cut or not wear them in potentially dangerous situations, especially around machinery," says Dr. John Bilos, an orthopedic surgeon at Chicago's County Hospital. "These accidents are totally preventable. All you have to do is have a jeweler make an oblique cut through the bottom side of the ring so that it breaks from the finger if it is snagged."

ROCK MUSIC

Rock performers are some people's witch doctors, and it doesn't take long for the bands to whip an audience into a frenzy.

Bottles and fists fly at rock concerts, and when an angry or adoring crowd rushes toward the stage, fans become a violent mob. If you sit near the exit door, you may avoid being a rock casualty, but there is no escape from the dangerous volume of the music or from the light shows.

Amplification experts agree that rock music is hazardous to hearing and not just at the ear-blasting volumes of concerts. Chinchillas' ears suffered terribly when scientists from the National Institute of Neurological and Communicative Disorders and Stroke escorted several of the animals to a disco.

Concert halls and, again, discos, are also bombarded by laser beams, the powerful waves of light that can burn through steel. In terms of its effects on the human eye, a one-milliwatt laser beam is nine times as intense as direct sunlight; sweeping through a crowd as part of a spectacular light show, such a laser is capable of burning skin, frying eyeballs, and igniting chairs, clothes, and walls. Lasers can also interfere with aircraft controls, an obvious danger at outdoor rock concerts. Light shows are dangerous spectacles—only engineers can ensure that their thrills don't kill.

RUGS

Carpets and rugs are the underlying cause of over 20,000 household accidents every year. What's more, the industry runs about a 40 percent "non-compliance rate" with government flammability standards.

RUNNING OUT OF GAS

This can lead to hitchhiking, which we know is a dumb and dangerous thing to do. A lot of people who run out of gas wind up siphoning a small supply from the tank of a samaritan motorist. A nice old trick, but it's difficult not to swallow the fuel, and very easy to get sick when you do.

Gas lines at service stations are not occasions that everyone uses for napping, knitting or reading—no, tempers flare as the pumps dribble out the nation's supply of fuel, and people have been shot for cutting in line. If you choose to brave a gas line, though, remember to turn off the car: an idling engine produces lethal carbon monoxide.

S

SADOMASOCHISM

Since S/M games are usually played under the influence of drugs (wrongly assumed to be aphrodisiacs), pain thresholds are easily misjudged and the climaxes of these sexual theatrics are likely to be reached in emergency rooms. S/M accouterments, odd arrangements of steel and leather that recall chastity belts, are readily contaminated by venereal germs.

SALT

Salt was once used sensibly—as money. That was before people got hooked on it as a flavoring, additive, and preservative. The Japanese and Americans shake more salt than anyone and the high incidence of hypertension in the two countries has a lot to do with all that sodium chloride consumption.

Salt has a good image—the salt of the earth, and all that—which continues to obliterate its dangers. Salt even creates something like dependence: Low-salt regimens are among the hardest for dieters to adjust to.

Snack foods are heavy in salt, and it's added to other products almost as much as sugar. It can create an excess of fluids in the body, which some people have great difficulty eliminating. Some coaches still pop salt tablets into their athletes, which is an idiotic thing to do—they feel like they're burning holes in your stomach.

The information can't be gotten from labels, so The Center for

Science in the Public Interest has issued a list of the sodium content of common foods. From that list:

1 apple—2 mgs.
3 oz. ground beef—57 mgs.
1 tbsp. Heinz mustard—213 mgs.
1 oz. Wonder potato chips—220 mgs.
2 slices Wonder bread—297 mgs.
4 oz. Del Monte tomato juice—320 mgs.
1 tbsp. Wishbone Italian salad dressing—362 mgs.
1 oz. Nabisco Wheat Thins—370 mgs.
1 Oscar Mayer beef frank—425 mgs.
½ cup Jell-O instant chocolate pudding—486 mgs.
2 oz. Kraft processed American cheese—890 mgs.
10 oz. Campbell's tomato soup—950 mgs.
1 tbsp. soy sauce—1320 mgs.
1 (17 oz.) 3-course Swanson frozen turkey dinner—1735 mgs.

SEA SNAKES

> The many men, so beautiful!
> And they all dead did lie:
> And a thousand slimy things
> Lived on; and on did I.
> —"The Rime of the Ancient Mariner"

The world doesn't have many venomous marine reptiles, but among them is the formidable sea snake, and he is quite enough. Some sea snakes pack a venom that is fifty times more deadly than the King Cobra's.

The sea snake is hopelessly water-borne (they can hardly wriggle on land), and only one freshwater variety is known, in a Philippine lake. The snakes are fond of river mouths, harbors, and bays—unfortunately, places where we would be likely to fish and dive. Found primarily in the western Pacific and Indian Oceans, and along the west coast of Central America and Mexico, the air-breathing sea snakes grow to an average length of 4 to 6 feet. Their slender bodies end in a paddle of a tail which facilitates great swimming; they scoot frontward and backward with equal speed and grace, float for long periods, and can remain submerged for hours.

Sea snakes like to swim en masse, and many a nervous captain has sailed his ship through great coils of them. An obscure account describes a solid mass of sea snakes, twisted thickly together for some 60 miles at a width of 10 feet.

Their bite is painless, so you may not associate sea snakes with your aching body, a slowly ascending paralysis and lockjaw, and nausea. Other symptoms are drooping eyelids, weak pulse, difficulty in speaking and swallowing, great thirst, convulsions, and shortness of breath. Death is practically inevitable.

SKATEBOARDS

The Consumer Product Safety Commission estimates that 150,000 people are injured every year on skateboards, and ranks the "toys" as the 16th most hazardous product in the United States. Most accidents result in arm fractures, though 25 deaths were recorded by 1978. Pedestrians, motor traffic, and city sidewalks are to blame for the skateboard disaster—and, of course, daredevil sidewalk surfers, who now number about 20 million.

Only bicycles, the perennial number-one hazard, account for more accidents on toy wheels, but no wonder: They outnumber skateboards four-to-one.

SKYDIVING

Parachutes look like jellyfish. That should tell you something. Manuals say the minimum altitude for "safe" skydiving is 2,200 feet, but there is no such thing as a safe altitude. When, or if, the chute opens, the skydiver is yanked upward with a force that can do severe damage to neck and back vertebrae, and chutists are lucky not to get tangled in cords or collide with fellow free-falling fools. Too, wind currents are unpredictable: You may jump squarely over a pasture, but come to a brutal landing on a craggy coastline. (*See* BALLOONING, FLYING, HANG GLIDING.)

SLEEPING

There's no more perilous time of day than the hours you spend sleeping (eight if you're lucky). A few people are shark-like in their sleep requirements, while most spend a third of life oblivious to dangers that don't doze, including the nocturnal prowlings of criminals and critters. Too, sleep and dreaming, far from being relaxing, can rack mind and body. But so can the lack of sleep, so you're doomed if you do, doomed if you don't. There are a few things to keep in mind before you turn out the light:

—Fruit flies have been known to crawl up a sleeper's nose and lay hundreds of eggs inside his/her head. Once the flies hatch, they make the brain their feeding ground.

—Rats prefer to attack people in bed.

—Many old pajamas contain TRIS, the cancer-causing flame retardant.

—When people cannot sleep, they tend to battle insomnia with various sleep-inducers. Each year in America, 20,000,000 prescriptions for sleeping pills are written, a fourth of them for barbiturates. They're effective in causing drowsiness all right, but aren't safe. (Barbiturates, especially pentobarbital [Nembutal] and secobarbital [Seconal] are widely used drugs of suicide.) Over-the-counter sleeping preparations are neither safe nor effective.

—Milk and meat contain an amino acid that seems to hasten sleep, but milk and meat hold their own horrors.

—Some people sleep in water beds which, in conjunction with electrical wiring, are death beds.

—Half of heart attacks and many strokes occur during sleep, and the

Sudden Adult Death Syndrome is the mysterious incidence of slumberous suffocation.

—Mortality rates are higher for people who sleep ten or more hours per day. (*See* TRIS.)

SMOKING

The correlation between cigarette smoking and emphysema, bronchitis, lung cancer, and heart disease is not speculative, it is real, and it is on account of tar, the most lethal component of cigarette smoke. Whether it's an unfiltered Lucky Strike or a Carlton doesn't much matter because people tend to smoke a greater number of and draw more deeply on low-tar cigarettes. Worker absenteeism of smokers is twice the rate of non-smokers. (But maybe that's a blessing—see WORKING.)

A cigarette doesn't have to touch your lips at all to hurt you. "Passive smoking" is what non-smokers are forced to do in the company of smokers, and it may not lead to lung cancer, but does interfere with oxygen's journey to the heart.

SNAILS

Just because something is spineless doesn't mean it can't hurt you. Snails are second only to mosquitoes in inflicting tropical parasitic diseases, schistosomiasis claiming a number of worldwide victims equal to the population of the United States. The cause, and namesake, of the disease is the schistosome, a flatworm whose larvae live in several species of the slow-motion mollusks. Irrigation projects, canals, river developments, and reservoirs have provided new habitats for a variety of snails and one species, *Tropicorbis obstructus,* has arrived in Florida, a trouble-making stowaway of the tropical fish trade.

When people splash around in schistosome-infested waters, the larvae are given the opportunity to burrow inside their bodies, accomplished in a flash, and the things grow there into worms, mate, and lay loads of eggs in the blood vessels, bladder, and intestines. The eggs are carried in the bloodstream to organs throughout the body, even into the brain. Many worms take up permanent residence in humans, producing thousands of eggs, year after year. When eggs are passed out, they enter snails, and begin the process all over again.

Appropriately enough, schistosomiasis causes sluggishness, and, though the disease isn't necessarily fatal (amazing, with those worms invading so many vital organs), it pretty well wastes the body. Drugs prescribed to treat the disease—like the substances required to exterminate the snails in their natural waters—have highly toxic side effects.

SNAKES

Opbidiophobia is a well-founded fear. The only thing to do as far as snakes are concerned is to move to the West Indies or to New Zealand, where for some wonderful reason there are no venomous serpents. (The only other heartening news about snakes is that many of them feed on rats.) Other than those islands, the two hundred species of snakes dangerous to man have a distressingly broad range and Roger Caras figures that they kill more people in one year than sharks do in one hundred.*

In the Old World and the New, people have expected a great deal from snakes: wisdom, holiness, evil, portents of death, everlasting life, libidinal arousal. In ancient societies, they were an honorable means of suicide: The ''asp'' beckoned by Cleopatra was more likely a cobra. The worship of snakes has gotten people nowhere, but the creatures do not deserve persecution either. Left alone, snakes will lie low, and concentrate on those rats.

Gardening, stalking Amazonia, camping, or taking up residence in a village in India, people tread upon the snakes' world and must face the great risks thereof. Composed of not much else than muscle and bone, poisonous snakes—long or short, fangs front, back, or retractable—inflict bites that feel like jabs of hot needles.

The toxicity of a venom varies, but North America's deadliest

*Roger A. Caras, *Dangerous to Man*. New York: Holt, Rinehart, Winston, revised edition, 1975,

belongs to the rattlesnake. Rattlers, whose fangs plunge through muscle, veins, and arteries, account for 90 percent of fatal snake bites in the United States. Texas, Arizona, Florida, Georgia, and Alabama report the most rattler bites, but the snake's ground extends from Canada to Brazil.

India regularly records between 15,000 and 20,000 fatal snake bites per year, or about two-thirds of the world's total. While rattlers are not found in India, cobras and mambas are, as well as in Hong Kong, Burma, and in parts of Africa. The King Cobra's venom is unimaginably potent, and since the snake can grow to a length of 20 feet, it might simply frighten people to death. Another species of cobra can spit venom 10 or more feet with amazing accuracy, temporarily blinding victims so it can move in for a direct hit. Mambas and puff adders are exceptions to the rule that snakes avoid humans—the adder chooses to occupy areas of human habitation, and mambas will actually chase people.

Snake venom has various effects, ranging from the utter destruction of tissues at the point of entry to a direct interference with the body's vital functions. Death from venomous species is usually a painful (though mercifully quick) affair—and probably beats being slowly strangled or swallowed by a python. (*See* CAMPING, JULY AND AUGUST.)

SOCCER FANS

Soccer is a simple, uncomplicated game—primitive, you might say. Aficionados say it's the game with everything: speed, skill, drama, and danger. That element of danger has become sufficiently frequent to obliterate the joys of the game, and its fans, easily the most violent in the sports world, are mostly to blame. The world's soccer fans have never been shy (a disputed goal in Kayseri, Turkey brought out pistols and knives and left 41 people dead), but they're particularly demonstrative in Latin American countries. In South America, a new slot for "Fatalities" might well be added to scoreboards at soccer stadiums.

One of the world's oldest sports, soccer is also the most popular in Latin America, and the games are big events in people's lives. They bring everything they've got to the war games: high hopes, soaring excitement, national pride, and pent-up aggression. For at least the past decade, Latin American soccer fans have taken the laws of the game, and of the land, into their own hands, storming playing fields when things don't go the way they'd like. It's gotten so bad that some playing fields are separated from the stands by fences or even moats.

Any way you look at it, soccer fans behave atrociously. Sample these briefs from *The New York Times:*

Montevideo, Uruguay, August 1, 1972. Four spectators shoot two soccer players to prevent them from scoring a goal.

Brasilia, June 18, 1973. Soccer referees protest fan violence—forty games cancelled.

Teresina, Brazil, August 28, 1973. Four crushed to death, over 100 hurt when panic breaks out at soccer match.

Mexico City, December 16, 1973. One killed, 100 hurt in riot following soccer game.

San Pedro Sula, Honduras, March 17, 1974. Thousands of soccer fans burn down stadium when matches are called off due to hostile crowd.

Belem, Brazil, May 2, 1974. One killed, three wounded at soccer match riot.

La Paz, Bolivia, October 3, 1975. Five wounded in fight between soccer games.

La Plata, Argentina, December 4, 1975. Angry soccer fans set fire to stadium.

But the worst happened in Lima, Peru on May 24, 1964. Fifty-three thousand had crammed into National Stadium for Peru's playoff with Argentina for the Tokyo Olympics. Tickets had been sold out for weeks, and a large, rowdy group of shut-outs crowded outside the stadium.

According to eye-witnesses, police, accustomed to trouble at soccer games, lined the perimeter of the field, over-armed with truncheons, tear gas, and even pistols. The first half went off without violence, and with no score. Adrenaline was pumping as the second half began.

Argentina finally scored a point. When Peru quickly matched it, a referee disallowed the point, calling a foul against Peru. An enormous outcry from the stands, then glasses, rocks, and bottles. Police clubbed a man as he scrambled over the 9-foot fence surrounding the playing field to lunge for the referee.

Fearing the crowd's mounting rage, officials called off the game, an announcement that sent scores of spectators to the fence, which they destroyed enough of to allow hundreds to spill onto the field. Police met them with clubs and held others at the fence with tear gas. Fires were started in the stands, and fans demolished whatever they could: seats, railings, lights.

Perhaps the riot would have exhausted itself if the police hadn't made their next move. Suddenly, they began to throw tear gas grenades into the stands, although that crowd was basically under control. Thousands gagged at once and blindly rushed toward the exit gates. Hundreds were trampled, and three police were killed in the mob. The massive steel doors at one end of the stadium had been closed to contain the riot, so the panicked crowd that rushed toward them was soon a horrible pile of people. As they climbed on top of one another, pressure mounted on the doors which finally burst open, crushing those on the outside. Bottles and other missiles flew, cracking heads and drawing blood.

The awful mob of police, fans, and players finally dispersed, all in a state of shock. The casualty toll of the Lima soccer riot was what you might expect from a natural disaster: 328 dead, 1,000 injured.

SOFT CONTACT LENSES

Soft contacts are susceptible to bacterial invasion, which, depending on the bacteria, may lead to blindness. Of course, hard contacts can cut the eyeball and glasses can shatter, so you ought to just put up with being nearsighted or farsighted.

SOUTH AMERICA

South America is the home of more civil wars, coups d'etat, and assassinations than any other continent.

It is also where the Amazon flows, from the Andes north of Lima to the northern coast of Brazil. The climate along much of the Amazon's 4,000-mile length is unpleasant and unhealthy, and the river itself is infested with crocodiles, boas, electric eels, and piranhas.

And don't forget the soccer fans.

SPACE FLIGHT

Unmanned satellites are the right idea, for outer space is no place for human beings. Better to stay on earth where meteorological, physiological, and psychological hazards are at least bound by the same laws that govern you.

Star-trekking initially requires escaping earth's gravity at 25,000 mph, a thrust that can burst capillaries, inhibit muscular movement and respiration, and cause facial distortions that could scare you to death. Subsequent deceleration exerts violent pressures on the body's internal organs. Weightlessness, the normal condition of space flight, creates muscle tension, and may bring on sinus and respiratory disorders, since exhaled carbon dioxide, dust, and exhaust from sneezes tend to hover in the astronaut's face. Weightlessness also reduces tactile sensation, so you could very well burn or freeze to death without ever knowing what was happening.

Time becomes meaningless in space, something that should be rather nice, but the imposition of an artificial day/night cycle inflicts insomnia, anxiety, and bowel irregularities.

Out in space, there is little to protect you from microwaves, cosmic rays, starbusts, and radiation that can coil chromosomes and contaminate a ship's food supplies—and absolutely nothing to protect you from being crushed by a meteor. Should a meteor puncture the spacecraft, or the cabin's delicate atmosphere controls fail, an abrupt change in pressure would ensue, either blowing you out into the void, compressing you to the size of a pea, or triggering a number of gas-related maladies, including abdominal cramps, neurocirculatory collapse, hemorrhaging, brain damage, and actual destruction of body tissues.

Boredom and loneliness are particularly stress-producing in space, where diversions are limited. On projected long-term missions with large crews, you'd be dependent on people dressed just like yourself for cooperation and companionship—the same people you'd fear in the event of an infectious disease that would whip through a ship's closed community in no time. The ultimate danger of space flight, of course, is the chance of meeting up with bacteria or beings against whose violence and/or intelligence we would be defenseless and/or dumb.

Getting back home isn't easy. Re-entering any planet's orbit is tricky business; if the angle of the red-hot craft isn't just right, it will be deflected and sent bouncing through space for eternity. (*See* BLACK HOLES, METEORITES, NOVAS.)

SPELUNKING

Think of caves as the ongoing destructive geologic processes that they are, and their dangers will be abundantly clear. Only luck has kept down the number of spelunkers trapped in cul-de-sac passageways, impaled by falling stalactites, and crushed under cave-ins. Caves tend to be easy to enter but difficult to get out of, sort of like romances; when this happens, spelunkers face attack by spiders, starvation, or suffocation (oxygen is not plentiful in caves). Nor should the hazards to health posed by bats and their guano be overlooked. There are over 900 species of the flying mammals, and they can transmit almost as many diseases as rodents.

SPOTTED POTATOES

Green or mauve spots on the leaves, petioles, and stems of potato plants indicate "late blight," the fungus disease that so devastated last century's harvests in Ireland that 30 percent of the island's population died of starvation within a 15-year period.

The fungus also attacks tomatoes, but it's scarier when the blight botches potatoes, for the tubers are important to many nations for their carbohydrate, vitamin C, and thiamin value.

STAIRS

Stairs are second only to bicycles on the Consumer Product Safety Commission's hazard index. Every year, a half million people tumble from steps, ramps, and landings. These statistics once again prove the rampant clumsiness of Americans, so why invite injury by living in anything but ground-floor dwellings? (*See* HOME.)

STEROIDS

Steroids are a group of natural and synthetic organic chemical compounds that include venoms and, more subtly dangerous, hormones. Hormones are amazingly powerful and multi-purpose: They rev up respiration, heartbeat, and perspiration; raise blood sugar level; slow down digestion.

Vaginal cancer occurred in so many teenaged daughters of women who took diethylstilbestrol that the synthetic estrogen was finally banned. (About two million women were prescribed the hormone, which was thought to prevent miscarriages.) Oral contraceptives, steroids themselves, are linked to high blood pressure, strokes, and blood clotting. (*See* THE PILL.)

The worst news from the strange world of steroids is hormone abuse—androgen, testosterone, and estrogen for kicks. Kids on hormones plunge into metabolic confusion, retarding puberty, and throwing sexual dimorphism out of whack. The biological chaos of hormone-popping subsides, but the possible identity crisis may not.

SUBSIDENCE

People in Dallas say there's good news and bad news about Houston. The good news is that their rival city is sinking, the bad news that it's not sinking fast enough. Actually, Houston is sinking plenty fast, an alarming 6 inches per year in some areas, and it's not the only city losing height. Land subsidence could predicate major disasters in such population centers as London, New Orleans, Las Vegas, California's San Joaquin Valley, Tokyo, and Mexico City.

Subsidence is usually gradual, but can be catastrophic. Houses, drilling rigs, and factories have suddenly fallen into sink holes. If cows and cars may be the fateful weight that triggers collapse of fields and highways, then skyscrapers are surely next to be swallowed by the earth.

Various kinds of mining and drilling operations contribute to subsidence. Its main cause, though, is water depletion, which is really bad news, being costly and difficult to correct. Basically, water is being pumped out of the ground faster than it's being replaced, and water demands can only grow. Rampant water usage is leaving a powdery mix of silt, sand, and clay beneath farms and cities. Farms and cities are heavy, so they're depressing the land, below sea level in some cases.

Venice has employed an elaborate system of aqueducts in an attempt to stop sinking while Houston and New Orleans have devised miles of canals to bring water into their precarious subterrains.

Meanwhile, one needs to walk softly.

SUBURBS

Two of the chief rationales of suburbs—their distance from city crime and the relief they offer from the pressures of urban living—are no more. Suburbanites are in fact more vulnerable than city dwellers, for suburban social maladies may go undetected indefinitely.

Vandals are terrorizing suburbs, and their favorite weapon is the common air rifle, which has a velocity of over 300 feet per second. The rifles are perfectly legal; dads and uncles like to buy them for their sons and nephews who then load them with BBs, pellets, or even darts, and roam from lawn to lawn shooting out windows and eyes. Marauding teens have also taken to shopping malls where they congregate for parking lot drag races and muggings.

Despite the widespread use of drink, drugs, and bank loans, despair is up in suburbia. The grim fact is that the suburban suicide rate continues to rise year after year.

SUBWAYS

Cities with subways have surprisingly low crime rates, so the millions who ride underground (over 3,000,000 passengers daily in New York alone) are not so much threatened by their fellow passengers as:

—turnstiles that jam and cause serious abdominal injuries;
—so-called safety doors that don't always do what they're supposed to do, that is, keep the train at the platform if they've slammed shut on any clothes or arms;
—the new systems, such as San Francisco's BART (the worst place, incidentally, to be during an earthquake) and Washington's METRO, whose sterile design, deadly silence, and cold efficiency numb human reflexes.

Liquefied natural gas (LNG) is the greatest subway hazard. In its vaporous state, natural gas is not easily transported, so its sellers "freeze" it into a liquid in order to ship it all over the world by rail, truck, and barge—without question, the deadliest cargo going. Heavier than air, escaped LNG hugs the ground and sinks into basements, sewers, and subway systems. The supercold liquid flash-freezes everything in its path, instantly destroying any living tissues it comes near. Shortly after a spill, LNG vaporizes, consumes oxygen (causing suffocation), and finally ignites in an explosive fire we lack the technology to extinguish. The fire, the likes of which are not seen in nature, would whip winds up to 1,000 mph. In 1944, 1.2 million gallons of LNG seeped from a ruptured tank in Cleveland, and blew into a fire whose center reached 3,000° F. When the fire finally burned itself out, 14,000 homes had been incinerated, 300 perople injured, and 130 killed. The city sewer system was largely destroyed.

An average truckload of LNG—9,000 gallons—would lick through 15 miles of subway tunnel, causing a horrible underground inferno, an unspeakable urban disaster. The fact is not academic: The world's largest LNG storage facility is on New York's Staten Island.

THE SUN

> Thank heavens the sun has gone in and I don't have to go out and
> enjoy it.
> —*Logan Pearsall Smith*

Time was when skin cancer was thought to be a disease of the aged, the
sad but practically inevitable fate of old hide. But that was before the
boom in leisure and recreational activity, when the droll began to loll
about so, and show-offs started to swim, ski, and surf with such
relentlessness. It was also before we realized that a myriad of pollutants,
from aerosols to jets, were eating away the sky's ozone. Ozone, of
course, shrouds the earth, and screens the sun's ultra-violet rays, the
ones ultra-violent to the human epidermis. The result of all this
nakedness under the sun is about 300,000 young and old victims of skin
cancer every year.

Burned skin wrinkles and dries and thickens and will never be smooth
again, for ultra-violet rays penetrate even tanned layers to continue their
attack. Damage from the sun can result in lesions and blisters, and
permanently burned eyes. (You can also soak up damaging ultra-violet
from sunlamps and "health club" tanning booths.) Keep leather in
mind—it's nothing but tanned animal skin, and you don't want to return
from the beach looking like your luggage.

SUNGLASSES

Sunglasses don't afford the eyes much protection, but, behind them,
people may feel immune to the sun's cancerous rays. This confidence
leads quite expectedly to the ravages of overexposure, including burned
retinas.

SURVIVAL COURSES

The ultimate challenge is to survive survival courses, which have
experienced an upsurge in popularity since the world has heard anew the
call of the wild. The best-known survival courses are offered by

Outward Bound's 34 schools, 7 of which operate in the United States. Survival course instructors, who exhibit all the qualities considered desirable in drill sergeants, teach their city-slicker students how to hurt themselves and others by building campfires (proudly, without matches), scaling cliffs, running rapids, and hiking for miles. The survival course regimen has resulted in at least one fatal heart attack.* (*See* CAMPING.)

SUSPENDERS

The slapstick turn of getting popped in the eye by a suspender strap is no joke. Another reason to wear belts is that suspenders give attackers, propellers, and fast-moving trains something to hold on to.

SWEETS

People are anything but frightened of sugar—the average American eats about two pounds of the refined white variety each week, over one hundred pounds a year. Most ten-year-old kids in the States get a third of their calories from snack foods, which are loaded with sugar. That's the trouble with sugar consumption: You don't have to sprinkle it to get it. It's expected in cookies, ice cream, and syrups, but it's also hiding in crackers, yogurt, and sauces. Sugar is absolutely the world's leading food additive.

There are some unproven charges against sugar—that it is addictive and the major cause of acne and hypoglycemia—but its proven dangers are quite enough to make you clamor for precise sugar-content labeling of processed foods.

The runaway consumption of sugar has caused a metabolic crisis. Full of empty calories, sugar is our stupid and major supply of energy-giving carbohydrates. Sugar itself cannot actually make you fat, but its presence tends to make you eat more and destroys your appetite for nutritious foods. High sugar consumption is linked to heart disease

*The fatality did not occur in an Outward Bound course.

(North America and Europe's number one killer), gallstones, varicose veins, back problems, arthritis, and high blood pressure. Sugar also seems to rob the body's B vitamins and interfere with calcium metabolism.

Sugar, especially in its stickier, candied forms, is famous for its own consumption of teeth. Bacteria in the mouth thrive on sugar, creating acids that ruthlessly attack enamel.

It's important to keep your "-oses" straight, and not be misled by "health" sugars. All sugars are natural products and one, fructose, from fruits and vegetables, is decidedly a nutritional improvement over sucrose, refined from sugar cane and sugar beets to white table sugar. "Raw sugar" is 97 percent sucrose and full of dirt, bacteria, and bugs. It's banned in the United States. When it's partially refined, raw sugar may be sold as "turbinado," and is no better than the bleached stuff. Brown sugar is just that—white sugar spray-painted with gooey molasses syrup. Since honey is concentrated, less is consumed, which is good, but don't think it's any healthier than white sugar. Saccharin, of course, is an artificial sweetener whose laboratory links to cancer should have it banned like its predecessor, cyclamate.

T

T-SHIRTS

Since advertisers made the curious discovery that people would actually pay to wear their logos and slogans, T-shirts have become probably the most ubiquitous and certainly the most mobile media for various products and services and politicians. Philosophies and lifestyle brag were soon adapted to the silkscreen process, and that's where the trouble began. Details aren't necessary: Just think of what could happen if someone doesn't like what your chest proclaims.

TEACHING

Teachers once instilled fear in students, but it's the other way around these days. Public schools have been called "jungles," which is more apt than ever, with students as ruthless guerrillas. The violence is almost unbelievable: 60,000 public school teachers were assaulted in hallways and classrooms in the first half of 1978. A thousand injuries each month require medical treatment. Students rape, beat, and shoot teachers. One teacher's hair was set on fire by an irate student. The National Education Association says that at least 6,700 public schools in the U.S. are riddled with serious crime problems, and that teachers are consequently suffering from something like combat fatigue.

Some school systems have even published faculty handbooks on self-defense and disarmament of students.

TECTONICS

If the earth would just hold still, it'd be a much safer place. The convectional movement of the great continental plates—geologists liken it to the rise and fall of froth on simmering soup—is a phenomenon of tectonics, and is responsible for most of the planet's destructive seismic activity. When tectonic plates collide, and this is an ongoing occurrence, the result is a sudden release of subterranean energy. We're talking about earthquakes, volcanoes, landslides, and tsunamis.

Some quakes are not tectonic in origin, such as those that have ripped through South Carolina and Missouri, but most do occur at the margins of plates; these include the global growls of Chile, Peru, the eastern Caribbean, Central America, southern Mexico, California, southern Alaska and its Aleutians, Japan, Taiwan, the Philippines, and New Zealand. Earthquakes not only swallow people and buildings, but burst water and gas lines, and jolt open wild animal cages. There are seven geological phenomena that, singly or in any combination, herald a major earthquake*:

1. slight changes in the tilt or elevation of land;
2. variations in the velocity of sound waves traveling through deep rock;
3. changes in electrical conductivity of earth's crust;
4. changes in configuration of the magnetic field;
5. large amounts of radioactive radon gas in deep wells;
6. changes in volume or temperature of water in deep wells;
7. increases in tremors.

One has to admire the fatalism of people who live in earthquake zones; perhaps they see some nobility in being swallowed by the earth. There is certainly no doubting quake power: One of the worst on record hit Shensi, China, in 1556, killing 830,000 people. A quake in Guatemala killed 22,000 and injured 75,000 in 1976. Less than 2,000 Americans have died in earthquakes, so our luck is now bound to be on the downslide, especially in California, southern Alaska, Hawaii, at the Arkansas–

*Source of seven warning signals: "Earthquake Forecasting," by Sandra Stencel, *Editorial Research Reports*, 1976, volume 2.

Missouri–Illinois–Kentucky–Tennessee border, upstate New York, and eastern Kansas.

Millions of people live in the shadow or on the slopes of the world's 741 active volcanoes, which rise from the edges of tectonic plates and whose eruptions all too often punctuate earthquakes. Volcanoes are main lines to the earth's molten, tempestuous core and, when pushed to the brink to tectonic disturbances, give nature's greatest fireworks display in the release of pressures that have been capped for centuries. The blazing juggernauts launch red-hot missiles, poison the air with carbon monoxide, and bury entire towns under ash and lava. Torrential storms usually follow volcanic eruptions, bringing floods and mudflows: The Krakatoa explosion of 1883 darkened the sky for seven days and caused a ten-foot rise in sea level. If a lake happens to sit atop a volcano, its contents contribute mightily to the deluge. When Crater Lake erupted in 1919, 5,000 Javans were killed under tons of water, ash, and steaming rocks.

"Inactive" volcanoes are about as safe as "unloaded" guns. Bezymianny, a volcano in central Kamchatka long believed extinct, blew 40 miles high in 1956. After it killed 30,000 citizens of Pompeii and Herculaneum in 79 A.D., Mount Vesuvius was inactive until it exploded in 1906, 1944, then again in 1953—and people still live in its path.

Often working in force with earthquakes and volcanoes, tsunamis are seismic disasters caused by sudden displacement of tectonic plates, or by landslides also of tectonic origin. (High winds can whip up a wall of water, but tidal forces cannot, hence, "tidal wave" is a misnomer.) Tsunamis may occur in lakes and reservoirs, but are most often the rage of oceans, particularly the Pacific. And how they travel: After engulfing a Chilean town, killing 2,000, a tsunami proceeded to rumble across the ocean floor, finally hitting Japan 22 hours later, where it leveled thousands of homes, sank hundreds of ships, and killed over a hundred people. As coastal areas continue to grow, the threat of tsunamis becomes more urgent.

Tectonics are surely the root of the most formidable geologic hazards.

TELEPHONE SOLICITATION

Telephone solicitors are trained to not be discouraged by simple "no's"—they'll try every angle in the book to sell magazines or appliances over the most personal and important medium in the house. The merchandising has had tragic results. Just as a young woman answered a call from a salesman, her mother had a heart attack. The daughter tried to hang up and get a dial tone, but couldn't and had to run next door to call an ambulance. An extreme case, but it shows what can happen when the telephone sales force starts ringing. Telephone solicitation is a nuisance, a dangerous nuisance.

TELEVISION

A television set is essentially a low-power x-ray machine that can zap your skin, thyroid, gonads, and eyes. High-voltage color sets are much more dangerous than black-and-white models, but both can do damage, particularly at close range. Radiation from television leaks from all sides of a set, so the only safe way to watch TV is to do so in a head suit, with specially treated glass over the eyes.

The theatre that most people set up for television is incredibly depressing and unhealthy. Entire rooms are arranged around the TV, like so many seats at the movies. The flickering set is often the only light in such rooms, and the set stays on, hour after hour, its immobile viewers virtually hypnotized into a stupor.

TIRES

Keep this in mind: If the car doesn't get you, its tires will. Firestone 500 Steel-Belted tires are no longer in production, good news that's come too late. Fourteen thousand accidents, leaving 50 serious injuries and 29 deaths, have been blamed on the tires' way of "unrolling" from the rim and winding around the axle. All in all, a terribly effective way for drivers to lose control of their cars.

Changing and inflating tires should only be done by trained people, and well-armored at that. Awful things can happen when a tire is accidentally punctured or over-inflated. Steel bands compound the hazards, since their fragments blow out of tires like shrapnel.

TOKYO COMMUTERS

Tokyo commuters don't just fidget and scowl when they're kept waiting. When late trains rumble into stations, the crazed Japanese commuters have been known to riot, bashing in windows, assaulting conductors, pushing fellow passengers onto tracks. People have perished in the platform pandemonium.

"TONIGHT'S THE NIGHT"

This Rod Stewart song advocates adolescent pregnancy even more crudely than Paul Anka's "Having My Baby." Stewart tells girls to shut up and lie down ("Don't say a word, virgin child . . . Don't deny your man's desire . . ."), and the song dissolves into an orgasmic chorus. A perennial rock favorite, "Tonight's the Night" no doubt inspires accidental pregnancies, had by one out of ten American girls every year.

TORNADOES

Without warning, the giant tunnels twist down from thunderheads, roaring louder than the Concorde, to do their damage quickly and completely. Nature's most concentrated force of wind and vacuum, a tornado can strike anywhere, any day of the year. About 600 hit U.S. ground every year (a record 960 struck in 1974), with an average annual death toll of 115.

Damage from tornadoes is not hard to imagine—what would you expect from 300-mph winds?—and can also take bizarre turns. Pieces of wood may pierce metal, buildings can explode, people and cars are blown about and returned to earth unharmed.

TOWNS

> People who make no noise are dangerous.
>
> —*Jean De La Fontaine*

With less than 50,000 people, a place can get spooky.

The much-touted quiet of towns is perhaps nice, but when broken it is done in the worst way, by vicious dogs, gregarious neighbors, crimes of passion, and little league fans.

Juvenile delinquency is growing faster in small towns than in cities, up 25 percent in some. These crimes range from burglaries (stealing pies from window sills) to assaults (beating people with baseball bats), and are compounded by the fact that there aren't enough people in small towns to hear you scream.

From time to time, the Ku Klux Klan rallies and recruits a few new hooded terrorists, almost always from small towns. A Klan appearance guarantees violence of some kind, if only between the warring factions of the KKK itself.

Small towns are also the originators of undesirable trends: The first McDonald's restaurant was opened in a small Illinois community.

TOYS

The bad news on toys is that they haven't changed much. They are still noisy, flammable, sharp-edged, explosive, poorly wired, mostly uninspired—and account for nearly a million accidents every year.

A couple of things have changed, however. Yesterday's sturdy, steel swing sets have been replaced by flimsy ones whose aluminum supports are less than an inch in diameter, the unsurprising result of which is that swing-related accidents have jumped to over 100,000 per year. (*See* ASPHALT.) Space guns and liquidators have joined western rifles and six-shooters in the early childhood arsenal. These sci-fi guns go zip instead of bang, and train kids to "pulverize" rather than "kill."

Then we have what are politely known as "adult toys," vibrators and cockrings, according to proprietors of sex shops, being the most popular. Vibrators may short-circuit or, worse, get lost. Cockrings are nothing new, although their invention, however misguided, was rooted in therapy rather than kink. Ancient Greek men probably weren't the first to experiment with a penile collar to maintain erection, a crude principle and a dangerous one: The throttle can cause gangrene.

TRENTO, ITALY

It's happened twice. The local lead factory in Trento, like all lead factories, is stocked with sodium which, if combined with water, forms sodium hydroxide in an explosive reaction. This particular factory leaks, so thunderstorms can, and have, caused huge explosions. The last one was in 1978, and had hundreds suffering skin irritation, nausea, and respiratory problems from toxic gas.

TRIS

Its use is now outlawed, but millions of garments out there are tainted with TRIS, the flame-retardant that causes cancer. Children's polyester, acetate, and triacetate pajamas were routinely impregnated with TRIS, but it was also used in industrial uniforms, wigs, tents, Christmas decorations, and draperies. None have been recalled. (*See* CHRISTMAS, SLEEPING.)

TRUCKS AND TRAINS

As the trucker barreled through Houston in his 18-wheeler, hell-bent on keeping the company's rigid delivery schedule, he wasn't thinking about his cargo. If he had, he'd have quit his job long ago, for he was pulling a huge tank of ammonia gas. It was 1977. Racing along the overpass of one of the city's busiest freeway intersections, something went wrong, and the truck tore through the railings and smashed to the ground 50 feet below. The tank exploded on impact, its contents a billowing yellow cloud of death. Trees and shrubs turned brown instantly, but thanks to Houston's weather which had prompted drivers in the vicinity to roll up their windows and turn on the air-conditioning, no one else was killed. The outcome could have been disastrous, as it was in Spain a year later, when a liquid propylene truck overturned near picnic grounds, its escaping gas knocking 200 people stone cold dead, and leaving 150 others with ravaged skin, eyes, and lungs.

Big trucks do not circumnavigate, but, thanks to interstate highways and the great freeway exchanges, haul straight through major cities. If their cargo itself is not dangerous, the noise, speed, and sheer mass of the trucks are. But the many shipments that do bear explosive or lethal materials, such as the truckloads of liquid natural gas making daily runs between New York and Boston, risk hundreds of thousands of lives.

No matter how ploddingly they move, trains are only as safe as the tracks they travel and their cargoes. Neither are. Until roadbeds and tracks are back in shape, trains will continue to derail and overturn. The slightest accident may have catastrophic results, since freight trains carry many of the same flammable, explosive materials as trucks, often in highly pressurized tank cars. When 20,000 gallons of epichlorohydrin spilled from 8 derailed cars in 1978, one man who ventured near the scene at Point Pleasant, West Virginia, wound up with massive health problems. Brief exposure to the deadly chemical, which is commonly transported by rail, is certain to cause lasting damage to lungs, testes, kidneys, and other organs.

TUG-OF-WAR

No one won the tug-of-war organized for 2,000 Pennsylvania high school students in 1978. The contest, intended as a break for the frazzled students during finals, was billed as an attempt to get into a book of records. They may have succeeded there, but for the wrong reasons. The long rope snapped, slicing through the students' hands like fine wire. Four lost fingers.

TUNA

Tuna fish is all but a staple of the American diet. But what's packed in all that oil and salt may not really be tuna. See, tuna fleets sometimes net dolphins, and if the mammals get processed, to resurface in sandwiches, salads, and casseroles . . . well, that's practically cannibalism.

U

UGANDA

Although Idi Amin Dada has ducked out for a while, his henchmen remain in Uganda and would welcome back their demented "President for Life." Amin is a savage man, an ex-heavyweight boxer who can be trusted, as they say, as far as he can be thrown. With its parliament abolished, Uganda is now a military state, its armies full of Moslem illiterates who do what "Big Daddy" tells them to do. That includes carrying out public and bloody execution of thousands of government officials, though Idi Amin's victims are often political innocents. Soldiers have killed individual youngsters and wiped out entire villages. In Uganda's ghastly prisons, inmates have been sledgehammered to death, and fellow prisoners have been forced to eat the corpses.

Idi Amin wants to erect a monument to Hitler. Having survived several assassination attempts, he thinks God is on his side. He has told his army thugs that if anything happens to him to "get your guns."

Uganda will not be a safe place for a long time.

ULTRASONICS

Ultrasonic waves are perceived not by ears but muscles, as they are used to produce deep-heat radiation in the relief of various somatic pain. About 40 million such treatments are undergone in the U.S. every year and, as is always the case with radiation therapies, overexposure looms as an unpleasant possibility. Patients of ultrasonic treatments have suffered burns and nerve damage.

UMBRELLAS

The modern umbrella, which dates from the 1700s, has to be one of the most foolish inventions ever, being as how they're used for protection against the rain of thunderstorms, which also produce lightning. Use a newspaper or wear a raincoat, for umbrellas are nothing but portable lightning rods. (*See* LIGHTNING.)

The basic design of umbrellas led to the invention of parachutes, which bear their own bad news. (*See* SKYDIVING.)

V

VAMPIRES

Vampires live, and in a family of mammals higher than bats. Oral sadists are people who, according to reports in *Archives of General Psychiatry*, get satisfaction from sucking human blood.

Castration complexes and aggressive hostilities (to say the least) are cited to explain the phenomenon. Whatever its cause, the psychosis is so complete that if vampires are unable to procure victims, they'll masturbate by noshing on their own veins.

VITAMINS

You probably never thought you could overdose on vitamins, but it happens to people with fuzzy notions of their power as preventives. The FDA has lifted limits once placed on vitamins A and D, and both, in megadoses, are toxic.

Excessive amounts of vitamin D can damage eyesight, encourage viruses and infections, weaken muscle and bone, and cause constipation, hypertension, skin eruptions, and mental deterioration. Vitamin A dries out skin and creates pressure in the head that mimics a brain tumor.

Amateur nutritionists advocate unlimited vitamin intake—A for osteoarthritis, D for osteoporosis, C to battle colds, B-1 for neuritis, E to prolong energy. An abundance of any of these vitamins can be harmful, and the danger becomes more apparent when you see vitamin preparations in stores that legally contain up to 32,000 percent of their recommended daily allowances.

W

WATER

The point is that we came out of the water 370 million years ago, and should only return to it, cautiously, for bathing, drinking, and doing the dishes. Water contains ripcurrents, piranhas, sharks, snakes, mosquito larvae, motorboats, and pollutants, all of which can kill you. Water-borne diseases, such as chlorea, have dealt more than their share of grief. Only things with gills or fierce-looking expressions, such as alligators, should dare go into water.

Even in its most civilized form, the swimming pool, water means wet death. Nearly 60,000 Americans were injured in various swimming pool accidents in 1977. Swimming pools are electrically lighted, filtered, and pumped, and not much needs to go wrong for all that wiring to send shocking currents through swimmers. Fiberglass pools are so slippery that people are more likely to fall getting in and out of them than the old concrete models, and chlorine in both is bad for eyes, skin, and hair. Should it vaporize from powder or liquid storage, chlorine could kill every swimmer and sunbather in sight.

Deadliest of all water is the tap variety, the stuff we commonly drink and cook with, and which contains, among other suspect compounds, PCBs, the chlorinated hydrocarbons which, studies indicate, cause sterility and mental disorders; chloroform; carbon tetrachloride; and kepone, the pesticide that decimated fish in the James River and caused neurological disorders in the people who manufactured it.

The National Health Federation says that fluoridated water correlates to high cancer rates, so fluoridation programs make water all the more frightening. Nearly half the U.S. population is drinking it; the District of Columbia has the highest concentration of fluoridated water, followed by Illinois, Colorado, Connecticut, Michigan, Minnesota, Maryland, Tennessee, Rhode Island, and New York.

Water-transportation services sustain the highest incidence of lost workdays—about 10 times the rate of all other industries.

Each year in the U.S., about 7,000 traffic fatalities occur on wet pavement.

Water rights have led to many violent feuds.

Floods

Floods are water at its worst, and their threat is not in the least remote. Twenty thousand U.S. communities are already flood-prone, and many cities are foolishly developing river frontage for commercial and recreational purposes. Talk about flirting with death: Floods, the most frequently declared federal disaster, are also the nation's number one natural killer. (Extreme cold actually kills more Americans, but those deaths are attributable to a variety of causes.)

Floods can happen in a flash; what seems like a simple thunderstorm can become a roaring river that rips houses from their foundations, knocks out utilities, and turns cars, trucks, and tractors into shipwrecks. An entire Chevrolet dealership in the Southwest was swept away by a flood in 1978 that also took 30 people.

But rain isn't the only source of floods, nor are rivers a requisite. Melting snow, ruptured glaciers, tsunamis (wrongly known as "tidal waves"), and sudden shifts of the ocean floor can all create the hydro-horrors. So can drought relief programs, which involve seeding clouds with silver iodine, a tampering with nature that has backfired with unheavenly rains. Cloud-seeding was blamed for the 1970 flooding of, of all places, the Arizona desert.

Floods are quite seasonal, striking the first half of the year, so we can at least be prepared to board arks. There is no other recourse; the marvels of water engineering—dikes, levees, by-passes, even major dam systems—are no match for the awesome power of floods, such as the Mississippi's in 1973 that covered 16 million acres, the Johnstown, Pennsylvania catastrophes that have drowned and marooned thousands, or the Black Hills flood of 1972 that left 237 South Dakotans dead and 3,000 injured.

Naegleria fowleri

Naegleria fowleri is the name given to an amoeba that kills most of the swimmers it attacks, as it's done in South Carolina, New York, Belgium, Virginia, and Australia.

The strange cell, identified in 1963, lives in murky lakes, polluted rivers, and clear springs. It enters humans through the nose, then travels the olfactory nerve into the brain, where it devours cells.

That's about all we know about it. A Florida scientist says that swimmers would be smart to wear noseclips or blow their noses after leaving the water.

(*See* POLYCHLORINATED BIPHENYLS, RED TIDES, SEA SNAKES, SNAILS.)

WEEKENDS

All hell breaks lose on weekends. People get depressed if they don't have anything to do, so are likely to drink as much as the ones out carousing. Highways get bloodier on weekends. Outdoor enthusiasts pursue the sports of their choice on weekends, risking heart attacks. Burglaries, assaults, rapes, and murders soar between Friday night and Sunday morning. And suicides are more likely to occur in conjunction with weekends, most being committed on Friday and Monday.

WOODEN CUTTING BOARDS

They're attractive and immensely useful in any kitchen, but wooden cutting boards can also be responsible for food poisoning.

Most livestock and poultry harbor salmonella, a group of rod-shaped bacteria that can tear up the human digestive tract. Before salmonella are destroyed in the cooking process, they may jump onto a damp and porous chopping block and thrive there.

Salmonellosis, commonly known as food poisoning, results in stomach pain, diarrhea, blood poisoning, and intestinal inflammation. In this case, it can be prevented simply by scrubbing the cutting board in hot water after each use, and letting it dry thoroughly. The new plastic boards are less aesthetic but also less hospitable to the bacteria, though some may survive in surface scratches.

Salmonella are no match for antibiotics, but you should be afraid of them, too. (*See* CAMPING, MEAT, PET TURTLES.)

WORKING

The wisdom of unemployment is abundantly clear. The workplace is booby-trapped with hazardous substances, mean machinery, stress, and poor safety regulations—so much so that one in eleven workers in the private sector suffers a job-related illness or injury. The rates are outlandishly high in construction, mining, manufacturing, transportation, fishing, forestry, and agriculture—and though these high-risk industries are usually very large businesses, 45 percent of workplace fatalities (as reported to the Occupational Safety and Health Administration) occur in small shops. Damage to and diseases of the skin are the most common job-related maladies.

About 20 percent of all cancer in the United States is contracted on the job, the consequence of inhaling, touching or swallowing any number of horrible things. Asbestos, for example, was once regarded as quite miraculous, an amazing fireproof material. Now it's got a disease named after it.

Over 800,000 tons of asbestos are used each year, in such products as theatre curtains, blankets, insulation, and ceiling materials. Painters, electricians, textile workers, carpenters, and machinists are among those plagued by its silky silicate fibers. Nearly 5 million shipyard workers were exposed to asbestos during World War II, and the National Cancer Institute has urged those men to watch for signs of asbestosis, lung cancer, and various cancers of the digestive system. Asbestos does its deadly work very slowly—it is not uncommon for symptoms to first appear 30 years after exposure.

Working for federal, state, and municipal government is three times as dangerous as working for private industry. After firefighting, garbage collection is the most hazardous public sector job, subjecting its workers to the harmful exhaust fumes of sanitation trucks, and hepatitis germs. Street and highway crews also suffer more than most workers. Meter Maids are frequently injured on the job and are often accosted by ticketed citizens—theirs has the highest accident rate of all city jobs in Boston.

In addition to physical harm, employment within any bureaucracy can cause extreme frustration and anxiety.

Here are some other livelihoods that could be the death of you:

Controlling Air Traffic

There are more relaxing jobs in the world than controlling air traffic. The Federal Aviation Agency says that air traffic controllers run twice the risk of developing hypertension as people who don't spend their working hours in airport towers simultaneously reading scores of radar signals in order to prevent runway and mid-air collisions. A traffic controller at Chicago's O'Hare, the busiest airport in the world, would really be a wreck.

Dentistry

Laughing gas (nitrous oxide) may have some not-so-funny effects. Suicide, most often committed by professional men, is most prevalent among dentists.

Doing Hair

Beauticians, according to the National Institute for Occupational Safety and Health, are more susceptible to chronic respiratory diseases and lung tumors than people who don't do heads. It has to do with their continual exposure to carcinogenic coloring agents and other harmful cosmetic products—which also include flammable hair sprays and toxic permanent-wave solutions.

Firefighting

When little kids say they want to grow up to be firefighters, they've opted for what's probably the most hazardous job in the world. The National Safety Council reports an average of 70 job-related deaths per 100,000 firemen, which is way above other public sector jobs, and 4 times the rate suffered by steel foundry workers.

Firemen routinely risk death from flames and smoke and aerial rescue maneuvers that are worthy of Barnum and Bailey. What's less known is the danger firemen face from depraved arsonists who snipe at them and booby-trap the buildings they've set afire.

In Memphis, however, you should be afraid of the firemen, who, when denied a pay bonus in the summer of 1978, set blazes around the city. It got so bad that the mayor declared a state of civil emergency, called in the National Guard and imposed a curfew until the incendiary firemen were doused.

Tax Collecting

Tax collectors aren't well-liked, and routinely get threats, obscene phone calls, and punches from taxpayers.

Woodworking

Of all the notorious manufacturing industries, lumber and wood operations are the most dangerous, regularly reporting some 20 mishaps (fatal and nonfatal) per 100 workers.

Violations of machine safety standards are largely to blame. The woodworker's tools are mean—saws, lathes, jointers, sanding machines, veneer cutters—and all their pulleys, knives, belts, gears, planes, shafts, blades, and electrical wiring must comply with regulations or more than wood will be ripped apart. (The roaring machinery is also ear-splitting, and produces tons of allergy-causing sawdust.)

It's hard to find veteran woodworkers with whole hands.

X

X RAYS

X rays smash molecules, thereby damaging cells which, if not readily replaced, embark on wild cancerous growth. X-radiation is extremely penetrating (only thick lead can deflect it) and is now joined by ultra-violet and microwaves in a relentless bombardment of life on earth.

The chief source of human exposure to X rays is the medical profession, but unfortunately, their diagnostic value is as immense as their potential for abuse. Until about 1966, X rays were in general use for arthritis, bursitis, spine ailments, fibroid tumors, tonsillitis, ringworm, and acne. Thomas Edison's fluoroscope machine was popular among pediatricians, since it enabled them to leisurely study young patients under an intense radiation that projected images on a sort of TV screen (a variation of this is used in airports to examine carry-on luggage). Dentists practically owe their livelihood to X rays.

Doctors have been wise to the side effects of X rays almost since their discovery in 1895, when German scientists reported that radiation treatments sometimes resulted in burns, blindness, or loss of hair—mild problems compared to what we know now. A series of famous tests in the 1950s and 1960s concluded that the effects of X rays are cumulative, and that the indiscriminate use of the fluoroscope had resulted in an upsurge of leukemia and other blood diseases in children. Leukemia was also discovered in newborns whose mothers were routinely X rayed during pregnancy. Dental and other head X rays have resulted in brain damage. If X ray–damaged sex cells are used in conception, offspring, perhaps many generations later, may suffer birth defects.

The intrinsic danger of X rays is compounded by the old, leaky equipment still in use today, and by the American Registry of Radiologic Technologists, whose standards are very low.

XYLENE

Xylene is a coal-tar distillate used in rubber cement, lacquers, aviation fuel, and in the manufacture of dyes, fibers, film, and cosmetics. Watery, flammable, and toxic, xylene can inflame skin, eyes, and mucous membranes.

Y

YOGA

To the ascetic Hindus, yoga is a means of attaining oneness with the universe, a union with the supreme being, liberation of the spirit, and all that. It entails a humorless life of self-denial, the basic non-activities of which being meditation, sitting in a contorted position, and abstaining from food, conversation, and sex.

To the great mass of non-Hindus, hatha yoga is a way of getting slim while watching television. Isolated from its cultural regimen, yoga exercise is not only meaningless, but foolhardy. The only thing Western devotees of yoga have in common with one another is backache. Orthopedists blame a slew of problems, from pulled tendons to slipped discs, on yoga, which has proven to be about as non-strenuous as pumping iron.

YOGURT

People who believe the mythology about yogurt—that it's a meal in itself—will starve to death. Low in calories and fat, yes, but the curdled milk is also low in everything else. A full cup contains only 25 percent of the U.S. Recommended Daily Allowance of protein and 2 percent or less of the U.S. RDA of vitamin C, niacin, vitamin A, and iron. The flavored varieties, the most popular, contain quite a sprinkling of sugar.

Z

ZEALOTS

There are two kinds of zealots: religious and not religious. Both share a passion for their own interests and a disregard for yours. From Aimee Semple McPherson to the Watergate burglars, zealots have been up to their shifty eyes in perfidy and profit. Religious zealots are the ones for your caution, for they say they know the truth (people who think they're right are the most dangerous of all), and they do know show-biz. They go around predicting death, preaching guilt, and encouraging the handling of poisonous snakes in rowdy, lunatic worship services. They also make a lot of money as they convert others to zealotry.

The hazards of nonsecular zeal were spectacularly demonstrated when religious arsonists set fire to an Iranian movie theatre in 1978, killing 377 people. But the most amazing thing happened the same year to a Utah family. The father believed he was the Holy Trinity so killed himself with carbon monoxide—the best he could do, we must assume, by way of crucifixion. His ardent wife had to follow him of course, but not before tossing four of her seven children from the balcony of their Salt Lake City hotel. The other kids blissfully jumped with their mom.

Religious zeal has a bloody past, and a future where more ignorant innocents will be misled, robbed blind, and sacrificed in some mighty perverse ways. Of course, the fanatics could be right.

ZIPPERS

Zippers will undoubtedly be in use when their invention is a century old in 1993, and they'll still be aggravating claustrophobia. The problem with zippers is that they sometimes do not unzip, and trap people inside trousers, sleeping bags, and tents. Zippers, therefore, are capable of effecting absolute immobility and isolation.

ENOUGH SAID

There are a few other things that are "mad, bad, and dangerous to know." (That's what Lady Caroline Lamb said about Byron.) They need little or no explanation.

ADVOCATES

AIRBAGS—their accidental inflation, which happens with a bang, could run you off the road

ALABAMA—has nation's highest general accident rate

ANAEROBICS

APHRODISIACS—rhinoceros horn is dangerous to procure and oysters are mercury-laden

ARMAMENT

ARMED FORCES FOR NATIONAL LIBERATION OF PUERTO RICO—terrorist group based in New York City

ARMED PROLETARIAT NUCLEUS—Italian terrorists

ARTIFICIAL FLAVORINGS—there are hundreds of them, many linked to hyperactivity

BAADER-MEINHOF GANG—German thugs

BASQUE HOMELAND AND LIBERTY MOVEMENT—violent politicos in Spain

BLACK SEPTEMBER SOLDIERS

BLUE LAWS—who's to say you won't need some life-saving product on a Sunday?

BLUE NOS. 1 AND 2—used in beverages, pet food, candy

BROMINATED VEGETABLE OIL—an ingredient in soft drinks, lodges in body fats

BUTYLATED HYDROXYTOLUENE—antioxidant in cereals, chewing gum, potato chips; a suspected carcinogen

CARBONATED BEVERAGES—they interfere with the body's assimilation of antibiotics

CARNIVORES

CATEGORICAL DENIALS

CHARISMATICS

THE CIA

CINÉMA VERITÉ

CITRUS RED NO. 2—used on skin of some Florida oranges

CLAWS

COMMON BOUNDARIES

CONGA DANCING—causes accidents where party-goers fall like dominoes

CONVICTIONS

THE COSMOS—an "ordered" universe is a misleading concept; it could lead on to
    assume that the void is friendly

COUNTER-ANYTHING

CRYOGENICS—thawing technology has a long way to go

CUBAN NATIONAL LIBERATION FRONT

CULTS

DEADLINES

DELICATESSENS—you can almost smell the nitrite

DEPILATORIES—whatever can remove hair can remove skin

DOSSIERS

DRILL SERGEANTS

EAR MUFFS—you need to be able to hear sirens

EDITORIALS

EFFERVESCENCE—in drinks or people

ENDEARMENTS

ENNUI

ESPRIT DE CORPS

EUPHEMISMS

FAMILY TREES

FLARING NOSTRILS

FLU SHOTS

.44s—turn back to handguns

FROTHING MOUTHS

GAS SPACE HEATERS—they gobble up oxygen, are the cause of many carbon
    monoxide poisonings

GLAZED EYES

GLEE

GREEN NO. 3—in candy and beverages

HALLOWEEN—costumes protect the identity of criminals; trick-or-treat has become a perverse adults vs. kids affair

HIGH SCHOOL

HISTRIONICS

HOOKAHS—any combination of water, smoke, and fire is dangerous

HORDES

IMMUTABILITY

INBREEDING

INFANCY

INTANGIBLES

IRA PROVISIONALS OF NORTHERN IRELAND

IRISH REPUBLICAN ARMY

ISLAND-HOPPING

JAW-WIRING—almost as dangerous as intestinal bypass as a drastic attempt at weight loss

LAUNDROMATS—you're a sitting duck for vandals

LIVER—it's good for you because it is the organ through which all things flow, but that's also why it's so bad for you

LOTUS POSITION—you may never get up; slumping in an easy chair is much safer

MACHISMO

MAFIA—feared since 1890

MANIFEST DESTINY

MARRIAGE—crimes of passion, stress, mortgages

MAXIMUM VELOCITY

MERCURY VAPOR LAMPS—the new lighting rage, energy efficient, but their breakage causes escape of large amounts of ultra-violet radiation

MEXICAN MARIJUANA—Random samples show that about 20 percent of all grass sold on the street is tainted with paraquat, the herbicide the U.S. and Mexican governments are using to eradicate those Mexican supplies. Damages lung and throat tissues.

MONOSODIUM GLUTAMATE—flavor enhancer in soups, seafood, poultry, cheese, sauces, many more. Destroys nerve cells in mice, can cause "Chinese Restaurant Syndrome," marked by headache, muscular pain, chest tightness.

MORTICIANS

MUTABILITY

NATURAL SELECTION

NECROMANCY—what you don't know can't hurt you

NEOPHYTES

NEW YEAR'S EVE

NIELSEN RATINGS

NIHILISM

NOMADS—they want your food

ORANGE B—used to tint the skin of hot dogs

OUIJA BOARDS—unless you're really willing to trust the future to the wisdom of a
    plastic toy

OVERACHIEVERS

OVERDRIVE

OVERKILL

OVERPOPULATION—there will be 15 billion of us by 2000

PARROTS—their beaks can tear out your eyes, and they also transmit psittacosis,
    a worldwide disease that will make you miserable for three weeks, and can
    even kill you

PEOPLE'S REVOLUTIONARY ARMY OF ARGENTINA

PHOSPHORIC ACID AND PHOSPHATES—used in many prepared foods, may cause
    osteoporosis

PLASTIC BAGS—seal in freshness, seal out oxygen

PLAYER'S CIGARETTES—the brand highest in tar

PLAYPENS—children get their heads trapped between the slats

POPULAR FRONT FOR THE LIBERATION OF PALESTINE

PORE PRESSURE—cause slumps, displacements, and slides of land; is main cause
    for collapse of hillside homes

QUAALUDES—you're usually much safer when standing up

QUININE—it's used to cure malaria, and also flavors some beverages, but it also
    may cause birth defects

RECALLS

REJECTS

RESTAURANTS—most food poisoning occurs as a result of eating out

RIZZO, FRANK

SAUNAS—high blood pressure, pulmonary aggravations

SCORPIONS IN THE SAHARA—they're huge and pugnacious

SELF-MADE MEN

SOUTH MOLUCCAN EXTREMISTS

SULPHUR DIOXIDE/SODIUM BISULFATE—used to prevent discoloration of dried fruit; also destroy vitamin B-1

SUNRISE—the dawn of another dangerous day

TATTOOS—the toxic dyes can pollute the bloodstream

TELEPHONES—their mouthpieces are also effective transmitters of disease

TELEVISION SHOWROOMS AND REPAIR SHOPS—unimaginable levels of radiation

TICKS—a New England tick produces a kind of arthritis in humans, causing skin lesions, crippling, facial paralysis, heart palpitations

TOMORROW

TRICKS

TURKISH PEOPLE'S LIBERATION ARMY

UNDERPOPULATION—then again, there could be too few of us by 2000, facing rotting surplus

UNFILTERED JUICES—these "health food" juices do not screen out flavorful pulp, or bugs

UPWARD MOBILITY

WANDERLUST

WHITE BREAD—chlorine dioxide, used to make flour look like baby powder, is toxic

WIVES' TALES

WOODSHEDS—home to spiders and snakes

YARDWORK—lawn mowers are one of the most dangerous products; critters don't like people fooling around with their habitat; heat strokes are common conclusions to gardening

YOUTH—most traffic fatalities befall those in the 15–34 age bracket.